Vinod Mehta's is an extraordinary story. He grew up as an army brat from a Punjabi refugee family in the syncretic culture of Lucknow of the 1950s—an experience that turned him into an unflagging 'pseudo secularist'. Leaving home with a BA third-class degree, he experimented with a string of jobs, including that of a factory hand in suburban Britain, before accepting an offer to edit *Debonair*, a journal best known for featuring naked women. With the eclecticism and flair that were to become his hallmark, he turned it into a lively magazine while managing to keep the fans of its centrespreads happy. The next three decades saw him become one of India's most influential editors as he launched a number of successful publications from the *Sunday Observer* to *Pioneer* to *Outlook*. Currently, he is editorial chairman of the Outlook Group. Vinod Mehta is the author of the bestselling biography of Sanjay Gandhi, *The Sanjay Story*, published by HarperCollins India in 2012. His much acclaimed memoir *Lucknow Boy* was published in 2011. In 2001, he published a collection of his articles under the title *Mr Editor, How Close Are You to the PM?* He lives with his wife Sumita, and dog, Editor, in New Delhi.

BLiTZ
Comprehensive Tabloid Weekly

"The most sympathetic, comprehensive and readable book on Meena Kumari"
—by K.A. Abbas

Few lives could be more fascinating subject of a full-length biography than the late Meena Kumari, renowned and exceptionally talented film star, poetess of sorts, incurable romantic, and the subject of much gossip and scandal which has not ended even after her death.

Vinod Mehta, the young author of the much-talked-about "BOMBAY—A PRIVATE VIEW", had one positive asset when he accepted the assignment to write the biography of the star—he had never met her. So he was free from the subjective associations, prejudices, preferences, complexes and inhibitions that would have beset any of the writers who knew her well.

The result is MEENA KUMARI (Jaico Publishing House, Bombay-1, price: Rs. 5|-), the first book to come out about the legendary film personality who died less than a year ago, almost immediately after the release of her life's most monumental success, "Pakeezah".

TWO WOMEN

Even if more books are published about Meena Kumari—and doubtless there will be—Vinod Mehta's "MEENA KUMARI" is likely to remain the most objective, the most sympathetic, the most comprehensively researched, and the most readable book on the enigmatic subject that will continue to intrigue and fascinate millions of her fans for many years to come.

To hear people talk about Meena Kumari, one gets the uncomfortable impression that they are talking about two totally different, and contradictory persons:

"She was a great actress—perhaps the greatest actress in the history of the Indian screen."

"She was a drunkard and an obsessive alcoholic."

"She starred in many tragic romances but the most tragic was her own romance and marriage to Kamal Amrohi."
"She betrayed and abandoned her husband."

"She was kind-hearted and gentle, generous and extremely helpful."

"She was in love with every hero she worked with."

"She was a truly genuine artiste in an industry dominated by fakes and frauds."

"She loved poetry and was a great and sensitive poet..."

"She was a poor versifier..."

"She was a saint..."

"She was a devil..."

Vinod Mehta's competent biography tells us that she was all these things, and NONE of them. She was a highly sensitive, highly intelligent, hard-working girl who worked all her life for others, and hungered for unattainable beauty and happiness for herself, who loved and lost, lost and loved again.

ROMANTIC

With restrained and civilised language (which our filmagazine gossip-writers, alas, will never learn) the author discusses her romance and marriage, her girlhood infatuation with the older person who came to be her husband, the estrangement, her other affairs of the heart and the mind, platonic and otherwise, the sadly lyrical romanticism that was a part or her life, the decisive influence of her helping hand in moulding several filmic careers, her inexhaustible hunger for love, for companionship, her isolation and frustration, but always her supreme devotion to her art and her work, culminating in the completion of "Pakeezah" and her tragic, untimely death.

It is an eminently readable story, told with sympathy and understanding, fair to all the participants in the drama of Meena Kumari's life and career, unconcerned with scandal, but never sacrificing the truth of Life which is more complex and more fascinating than any work of fiction. As told by Vinod Mehta, the greatest and the most romantic role played by Meena Kumari, the tragedienne supreme, was THE TRAGEDY OF HER OWN LIFE.

October 1972

MEENA KUMARI

Vinod Mehta

HarperCollins *Publishers* India

First published in 1972 by Jaico Publishing House

This edition published in 2013 by
HarperCollins *Publishers* India

ISBN: 978-93-5029-625-7

2 4 6 8 10 9 7 5 3

HarperCollins *Publishers*
A-53, Sector 57, Noida, Uttar Pradesh 201301, India
77-85 Fulham Palace Road, London W6 8JB, United Kingdom
Hazelton Lanes, 55 Avenue Road, Suite 2900, Toronto, Ontario M5R 3L2
and 1995 Markham Road, Scarborough, Ontario M1B 5M8, Canada
25 Ryde Road, Pymble, Sydney, NSW 2073, Australia
31 View Road, Glenfield, Auckland 10, New Zealand
10 East 53rd Street, New York NY 10022, USA

Typeset in 11/14 Weiss
InoSoft Systems Noida

Printed and bound at
Thomson Press (India) Ltd.

To Meena Kumari — wish I had known you

Contents

Nobody is perfect.

— Last line in Billy Wilder's *Some Like it Hot*

Acknowledgements to the Original Edition

He would be a brave, possibly foolish man who would write a book on Meena Kumari without the necessary escape clause. For myself, at every stage in the writing I found that it was impossible to collect even one 'undisputed' fact about this woman. Everything connected with her life had at least four versions. So I am sure lots of people will find enough material in this biography to complain, 'No, no, he's got it all wrong. It is not pineapple juice she liked but orange juice.' I have no defence against such complaints.

However, I am greatly beholden to the many people who made this book possible. To most of them I was a complete stranger—and film people are not over-renowned for welcoming strangers. Nevertheless, I was frequently made welcome and my queries were amplified and answered with patience and courtesy.

From among those who aided me, I would like to single out Mr Devi Dutt (Guru Dutt's youngest brother) who was of immense help. Arun Varma is the other person I would publicly like to thank.

Also deserving my thanks are those who supplied the photographs that illustrate this book. Mr Ramesh Madholkar, Mr Shiraj Chawda, Mr A.L. Syed and others who prefer to remain anonymous.

Finally, I must say thank you to my publishers. They accepted, without inserting a comma, my way of doing this book and gave me the sort of editorial freedom I frankly did not expect.

Vinod Mehta

Introduction to the New Edition

Meena Kumari died of cirrhosis of the liver (precipitated by excessive drinking) in March 1972. I was still working as a copywriter in an advertising agency, and going nowhere. With the false bravado which comes easily to a person who has achieved little, I accepted the commission from Jaico and duly delivered the finished manuscript in October 1972. The biography, published in paperback and priced Rs 5, appeared a couple of weeks later.

Meena's husband's magnum opus—*Pakeezah*—fourteen years in the making and vulnerable to the turbulence of their rocky marriage, had hit the screen in February 1972. *Pakeezah* opened at Maratha Mandir in Mumbai to a distinctly lukewarm response at the box office and from critics. Immediately after her death, however, a box office miracle occurred. You couldn't get tickets. The film became a roaring hit. Wild rumours abuzz at the time hinted that Kamal Amrohi had arranged the timing of her widely anticipated demise in order to rescue his tottering film. Homage to the famously tortured star was doubtless the prime reason for the film's reversal in fortunes.

I got a few good reviews, particularly from K.A. Abbas in *Blitz*, but I have to admit I was slightly embarrassed with my effort. Besides the subject of the biography being unavailable, I was ditched by the man who callously used and discarded her, Dharmendra. He gave me many appointments, none of which he kept. Somebody familiar with the film world said to me as a complaint, 'How can you write a biography of Meena Kumari without talking to Dharmendra?' True. Mr D was the love of her life. His absence from my script constituted a big void.

One other reason for my discomfiture. Because I was new at the writing game, I had few original or interesting ideas. The ones I did have were stolen, mostly from Mr Norman Mailer, who had not yet produced his tribute to Marilyn Monroe. Mailer's Pulitzer Prize–winning *The Armies of the Night* was all the rage in the early 1970s. In a sense he created a new journalistic genre, which allowed the author to place himself at the core of his narrative. It was a highly personalized rendering in which the word 'I' appears rather too often, while objectivity pops up rather too rarely. It still remained journalism but heavily author-centric. I lapped it up. At that formative stage of my writing career, my susceptibility to trendy literary movements and the fancy mode of expression of Anglo-Saxon writers should come as no surprise.

Although I have been an editor for nearly four decades, as a consequence of which my job almost on a daily basis involves grading manuscripts, I am a very poor judge of my own work. I need someone whose opinion I value to tell me whether I have written bullshit or a masterpiece. The feedback I got on my portrait of Meena Kumari went thus: I had produced an over-sentimental, maudlin life story compromised by the gratuitous insertion of my own personality into the narrative.

A cooler, detached view would have improved the biography immeasurably.

For the past ten years, more than one publisher has approached me with the offer of reissuing the book, with perhaps a fresh introduction. I have resisted the offers since I was not sure my biography merited the honour. Truth to tell, I had forgotten I had ever written such a book. More pressing matters—like learning the nuts and bolts of editorship—engaged me. Indeed, I did not even possess a copy of the book, neither did I know or care whether there had been a second print. The biography was part of my mediocre past.

After my memoir *Lucknow Boy* appeared, for the first time in nearly forty years I reread what I had written in 1972. All the solecisms and structural weaknesses were cringingly visible, but—how can I put this?—it was not as bad as I had thought. My self-created proximity to the subject posed an obvious and clear danger. Nevertheless, despite the naivety and exhibitionism and hurried judgements, I thought I had managed to capture some fleeting essence of the controversial actress. Was I being overgenerous to my own work? Perhaps. However, you must remember that in 1972 biographies of film stars were few and far between and those which existed were hagiographies. At least, I was able to puncture a few myths regarding the 'great tragedienne'. Most of Meena Kumari's multiple woes were self-inflicted as she convinced herself she was unfairly exploited and betrayed by her lovers and lady luck.

The 'great tragedienne', as the media called her, began to subscribe to her on-screen persona; it merged faultlessly with her unhappy real life. She fell for the oldest trick in the world. Meena considered herself to be uniquely cursed. And copious consumption of brandy provided the only relief. It is a delusion which many people, not just film stars, carry. Not surprisingly, without knowing much about her, she empathized greatly with Marilyn Monroe. The fact that Marilyn's husband, Arthur Miller, had some passing similarities to Kamal Amrohi, made the identification closer.

Mahajabeen Ara Begum (Meena Kumari), Fatima Rashid (Nargis) and Mumtaz Jahan (Madhubala) were contemporaries. While competition and rivalry must have existed between them, there is nothing to suggest the Katrina Kaif–Kareena Kapoor kind of petty bickering. When I spoke to Nargis, the actress was enjoying a fried egg on toast (she did not even offer me a glass of water!). She was entirely respectful and complimentary of her deceased contemporary.

How are Madhubala, Nargis and Meena Kumari remembered?

Nargis took early retirement after her marriage to Sunil Dutt, produced three children and became a social worker promoting safe causes. In 1980, she was nominated to the Rajya Sabha, where she took on Satyajit Ray. She accused the great auteur of giving India a 'negative image' by pandering to Western sensibilities. Nargis mounted a ferocious campaign to ban Satyajit Ray's films from being shown overseas, especially at film festivals. No one, including Ray, took much notice of her reactionary rantings. The lasting image of Nargis in the minds of most people is of the actress carrying an enormous wooden plough on her shoulders in Mother India.

Madhubala, by filmi standards, had a happy life—and mostly made happy films. Dev Anand remembers her as someone who was 'always laughing'. She was adventurous in her choice of roles, agreeing to play an Anglo-Indian cabaret dancer. Before doctors discovered a hole in her heart, she had a busy love life; she was two-timing Dilip Kumar by seeing

Premnath at the same time. A passing affair with Pakistan Prime Minister Zulfikar Ali Bhutto is supposed to have taken place. Because most of her films are light, frothy comedies—*Mr and Mrs 55, Chalti Ka Naam Gaadi*, etc.—with terrific music, she leaves behind a joyful ambience, although she had her share of troubles at the hands of her deeply conservative, bankrupt father.

In contrast, Meena Kumari, whose films are seldom shown on TV, evokes victimhood, pathos, despair and consistent bad luck. She played grief-stricken roles in which true love is found but only briefly. In movies like *Parineeta, Dil Apna Aur Preet Parayi, Pakeezah,* she either dies or is abandoned by her man. I suppose the mental picture of Meena Kumari which comes readily to mind is from Guru Dutt's *Sahib Bibi Aur Ghulam.* The scenes where she is seen pleading with her debauched and philandering spouse (played by Rehman) are unforgettable. He is trying to make her drink alcohol, something she abhors but consumes in the hope that her insobriety will persuade him to stay the night rather than visit upmarket brothels. *Bechari* is the word she is associated with.

I wonder what the new generation of under-thirty cinema-goers knows about her. They might possibly recall Nargis and Madhubala. But Meena who? I don't think I would have agreed, if some publisher had asked me, to write a biography of either Madhubala or Nargis. Meena Kumari was a diverting and more thought-provoking challenge. I am not sure I did justice to it.

May 2013

Section One

ONE

Lies

*If you have tears prepare
to shed them now.*

— Mark Antony in *Julius Caesar*

Pardon, but we are going to begin Meena Kumari's life story backwards—from her death. And if anybody I feel approves, nay applauds, this breaking of biography convention, it is the heroine of this book herself. For who better than her understood death, and who better than her played and toyed with it. I can nearly hear her confiding into my ear, 'Well done, Vinod, at least you got the beginning right.'

For me the beginning was at a party on a night which will presumably go down in celluloid history. Friday, 31 March 1972 was a serene, star-studded, breeze-laden night. The elements, almost in conspiracy, were determined to demonstrate that when they tried they could produce the right setting—not one of violent storms, angry waves, thundering clouds, extinguishing lamps (stock death symbols of the Indian cinema); rather a setting of softness and peace. I am

3

not exactly certain whether my heroine died in composure; what I am certain is that she died on a night of abounding and tantalizing tranquility.

The party—an open-air affair—was of some spurious distinction. Finely liveried waiters scurried around juggling glistening glasses of Scotch; bejewelled and bedecked women, often too fat and ungainly, sat mercilessly on weak chairs; shining-suit-attired men encircled the bar or moved about on the opulent green lawn. And in the background a band played *Pakeezah* songs—Oh! irony where is thy sting—while the smell of freshly cooked savouries delighted the nostrils. All seemed so well with the world.

The harbinger of death—and again how apposite—was a film star, a minor film star: the kind whose face was bitterly familiar but whose name one could not quite recall. He strode in with all the aplomb of a matinee idol. No fool, he knew this was his night (he was the only star around), and in this kind of party he stood, literally, alone.

Anxious, we men and women gathered around him, and I must confess he handled himself with some finesse and elan, though he was a little hurt when someone seriously asked him, 'Excuse me, what is your name?'

Rapt, we listened as he spoke about his current assignments, his past successes, his future plans. Someone, it appeared, was finally signing him on as a hero. You can't keep a good man down. He was going to make it right to the top. I couldn't help feel sorry for him as he tried to convince us that he was really a big star marking time for the vital break. There are, it occurred to me then, few things more ignominious and desperate in life than being a minor star. For I suspect his best and most creative energies are exhausted in establishing precisely the opposite, i.e., that he is not a minor star. (No need to tell my heroine this, she went through it all.)

Suddenly he stopped.

'Do you know Meena Kumari died this afternoon,' he informed more than asked. The response was staggering. Nobody said a word and for a few minutes it seemed everybody who had heard the news of the death was recovering not only from a shattering sense of shock, but from a sense of personal bereavement.

This response was not new to me. Serious and important deaths are received in silence; only the inconsequential demand weeping and gnashing of teeth. I remember when I first heard of Jack Kennedy's assassination I just stood rooted to the ground completely reaction-less. Similarly, that night we heard the news with a mixture of incredulity, shock and remorse which manifested itself in eerie silence.

No one I recall wanted to talk to the minor star any more. The group broke up and I heard tearful men and women commiserating with each other—proving, as if there is any need, that my heroine's loss was not Mr Amrohi's alone. For over two decades, to God knows how many men and women from the Himalayas to Cape Comorin, she had become a living and intimate symbol of all that was edifying and decent, venerable and noble, moral and righteous in the Indian way of life.

One of the paradoxes of death is that it demands explanations—and a mixed bag was offered that night: she was unhappy; she was friendless; she was drinking too much; she was unable to find true love; she was betrayed. And inevitably the final and subsequently the most accepted conclusion:

possibly she was better off dead than alive. What say you, Meena?

The obituaries were punctual. AIR in its nine o'clock bulletin carried the news of the death of the 'Well-known film star Meena Kumari'. The *Times of India* in an uncharacteristic gesture of generosity splashed a picture of the star on its front page. The *Hindustan Times* and the *Statesman* prominently featured the death; the *National Herald* wrote a touching third leader; only the *Hindu* seemed a little diffident in responding to the extinction of a North Indian film star. On page 7 of its 1 April issue it indicated, 'The late Meena Kumari was a Muslim who adopted a Hindu name when she became an actress.' The *Tribune, Patriot, Amrit Bazar Patrika, Indian Express, Assam Tribune* were all on the mark. If not in life, in death my heroine was front-page news.

Cinema halls showing *Pakeezah* flashed the news through hurriedly made-up slides. Maratha Mandir, Bombay's most prestigious hall, cancelled its last show; Mayfair in Lucknow, with an exquisite mixture of sensibility and sale, acknowledged the death and then decided that the show must go on. In Hyderabad, a handwritten poster outside the theatre did the trick: there were no empty seats that night. At Rivoli, Delhi, large crowds gathered in an already packed house (the fans rightly thought that if they couldn't see the film that night they could at least be near it). Only in Cochin was there no commotion—no one had heard of *Pakeezah*.

Meanwhile, the Bombay film world was choking with emotion and the gushing prose that emanated from Pali Hill, Bandra, Juhu, Malabar Hill, Napean Sea Road,[1] and countless

---

1 Localities in Bombay where popular film stars reside.

studios spoke in one voice of the incalculable and mortal blow struck by this untimely and grim death. Why, some of the more overcome producers decreed that shootings be stopped for a day!

The Ajanta Arts Welfare troupe (comprising Sunil Dutt, Mukesh, Sonia Sahni, etc.) sent this telegram from Jammu: 'While putting up a show for the families of the jawans we got the shocking news of Meenaji's death. It was a great shock for all. On announcement of the news at the show the public cried with shock. We observed one-minute silence with public.' Producer-director B.R. Chopra wrote, 'Meena Kumari is no more. It almost appears that, with her death, we are reaching the end of an era of great artistes dedicated and larger than life.' 'I have not,' conceded Satyajit Ray, 'seen most of her films but I saw her *Sahib Bibi Aur Ghulam* which impressed me. She was undoubtedly an actress of the highest calibre.'

Mr Rajendra Kumar thought that 'Meena Kumari was a sea of emotions, a treasure of human values'. Mrs Nargis Dutt emphasized my heroine's charm and grace. Miss Rekha, a film star, and Mr Tariq, chairman of the Indian Motion Pictures Corporation, said nothing in print. The former, however, burst into tears and had 'to be sent home immediately', while the latter 'rushed to the hospital'.

Raj Kapoor sent a cable from America; at the graveyard, Dilip Kumar lamented that 31 March 1972 was an unfortunate day since on this day in front of their own eyes they had seen helplessly the slow going away of a dear friend. David wanted her 'to rest in peace ... rest in peace'; producer Devendra Goel remarked, 'The way she used to express tongue-in-cheek humour or a deep emotion was simply stunning'; Mr Dev Anand concluded, 'Meena Kumari was the greatest artiste of them all.

…as no recognition of her histrionic talent.'
… confident that she would live for all time to
come; and Dharmendra had this to say, 'I learnt a lot from
her while working with her in so many films. An irreplaceable
artiste, her death was sad, but her life was sadder still.'

Fittingly, the only intelligent and perceptive comment
came from poet/lyricist Sahir Ludhianvi, '… an artiste with a
rare talent—a softspoken woman in white with the soul of a
poet had to sacrifice her childhood to start work before the
camera; her youth was spent in depicting various tragedies that
can befall an Indian woman, with no time to think of her own
personal tragedy. Her whole life was a sacrifice of her own
emotions, her personality, her own ego and their sublimation
in the art that gives joy to the millions. A cruel destiny put her
lily-white soul on the cross of human emotion.'

The film journals and their feature writers—for once given
an opportunity to 'write'—rose to the occasion with inspired
predictability. Solemn, big, thick, black borders encircled
pages of indistinguishable type. Anyone who knew an
adjective was commissioned. Bunny Reuben of *Star and Style*
observed, '… the fact of acting to her was an act of living,
like breathing. Like Paul Gauguin who just had to paint and
cared two hoots whether anybody recognized his genius …
one by one the giants are leaving the stage. And the pygmies
are taking over.'

Khwaja Ahmed Abbas (he seems to have written one tribute
for each journal)[2] believed that 'Martyrs never die. And it was
Meena Kumari the mortal human being that was buried in a
grave. Her soul, her art, is beyond decay.'

---

2 I have great respect for him otherwise.

B.K. Karanjia, editor, *Filmfare*, an exception, wrote some splendidly moving lines: 'She made a lot of money and lost it, she knew great love—and lost that too. Across those exquisite sculptured features, the marble made flesh, flustered the bemused query: "Is it true they say it is better to have loved than lost?"' Khushwant Singh confessed that he sat next to her and didn't know who she was (I suppose that's what happens when you sit next to too many famous people!), while an editorial in *Screen* lamented, 'It is sad that she passed away at a young age and at a stage in her career when she was maturing as performer of a variety of difficult roles.' Ajit B. Merchant in the *Bharat Jyoti* struck a refreshingly different tune as he explained, 'Despite the aura of melancholy around her name—a natural off-shoot of her fame as the screen's number one tragedienne—she could be extremely gay and exuberant.' Mr V. Verma came out with this gem: 'She had combined in herself two radical opposites, the grace of moghul-like living and the spontaneity of a hippie.'

Incontestably, the prize for overreaction must rest squarely on the shoulders of Mr Arjun Dev Rashk. In a long arcane piece titled 'You Died Manju So What' he had me guessing. He accused death (with a capital D), cirrhosis, himself, me and others for the departure of my heroine. In two climactic sentences—a sort of *'j'accuse'*—he howled, 'It is not the symbolical killer Tiger who turned killing into an art; It's you and I (swallow it you sons of bitches. Let us be men).'

The pride of place in this documentation of plaudits and regrets is reserved, naturally, for Kamal Amrohi. Sensibly, he said nothing about his departed wife as an actress, rather he spoke of his private loss in the form of an elegy: 'Once people took away my Manju after naming her Meena Kumari; Now this

cruel death has snatched her away from everybody; But I know
she isn't dead; She's sleeping in my heart in an immortal sleep.'

One doesn't necessarily have to be malicious or insensitive
or both, to suggest that all these carefully carved words were
ritual hypocrisy. Genuine grief, for even the gifted, is difficult
to express since it comes from the deep fathomless ocean of
the psyche. In this ocean words don't articulate easily and only
the heart knows the way. The sincerity of an obituary, one
may hopefully generalize, is usually directly in proportion to
its restraint.

So there may be something in the view that for a true
assessment of my heroine's death one may have to look towards
the less famous.

Look towards Bhawani Shankar, my servant: a philistine
fellow if ever, through whose breast a noble thought never
ventured. The day after Meena Kumari's death he requested
me if I could possibly have an early dinner.

'Why?' I asked.

'Sahab, I want to go and see *Pakeezah*.'

'But you saw it only last week!'

'I want to see it again,' he replied softly without meeting my
gaze. He was, I think, going that night to Maratha Mandir on
a pilgrimage. He was in effect going to lose Rs 2.50 and say
thank you to a woman who had become part of his life—that
is how the humble pay respects.

Or look towards Veena George of Secunderabad. Like
thousands of others she wrote an unsolicited tribute to one
of the film magazines. She pointed out that the day of my
heroine's death was auspicious and had a historical analogy.
Good Friday, she said, was a day of forgiveness and like Jesus
Christ 'Meena Kumari died on that day and I am sure she too

must have forgiven many of her so-called sympathisers who were really enemies of her life.' I find it easier to believe that the Son of God with his divine powers forgave his crucifiers; I am not too sure whether Meena Kumari did the same. 'Has she died? Has she been killed by her tormentors? Or has she committed suicide? Who knows? But perhaps all of us do know,' declared Jullundur's Radha Mongia.

Alternatively I think back to a devout-looking bearded taxi driver. He had stuck a picture of Sahebjan on his dashboard. I asked him the reason for this choice.

He had no reason except, 'Kya Aurat Thi' (what a woman she was).

There may be some depth too in what a Flt Lt Raj from Middlesex, UK, observed. He reprimanded the Indian medical profession for not looking after the physical health of stars. 'Otherwise how could such a young artiste die?' Mr Adam Esmail from Tanzania was relieved that Meena Kumari was able to complete *Pakeezah* before 'breathing her last. May her soul have eternal peace in heaven, the peace she never had in this world.'

I hope I am not being chauvinistic when I claim that the most telling reaction to my heroine's death came from my sister—a passionate and long-standing admirer. On hearing the news, she closed her eyes for a few seconds and sighed, 'Bechari.'

TWO

Birth

> *Give us a child for eight years and it will be a Bolshevist forever.*
>
> — Lenin

> *I never had a collection of bright coloured marbles like other children.*
>
> — Meena Kumari

Turn right at Dadar East railway station, continue thus for a few minutes, then walk through a crowded market bazaar, and if you persist in this direction you are likely to come upon an unpromising road called Dadasaheb Phalke Road. Everything around this road is both decaying and indestructible, and there is every reason to believe that five decades from 'Garibi Hatao' it will still be around. Both sides of the road abound with shops selling wares ranging from lungis to lassis.

Not far, on the right, is a building which, besides being colourless, pathetic and one-storey, is built to superb architectural imperfection. On the ground floor a few scanty stalls eke out a living while on the first floor there is a conglomeration of one-room, one-window tenements. In Bombay language such tenements are called 'chawls' and this one, spectacularly unfit for human living, is called 'Meetawala Chawl'.

'Where did Meena Kumari live?' I asked one of the boys standing around doing nothing. He considered me suspiciously and then pointed at a particular one-room, one-window. I absorbed the tenement for some time and I thought standing there, well it's right that one of the most famous and richest of women in India should have made a start from here. The rags-to-riches story certainly got its locale right.

My heroine's early home bristles with gorgeous overtones of irony. Adjacent is a large-gated Muslim orphanage with a long name, directly below is an entrepreneur who sells 'Indian and English eggs', opposite is a film studio, the Rooptara Studio, where the less important films are made. The boy who had helped me came and stood by me. 'Who are you?' he asked. I told him. 'Ah,' he chuckled, 'somebody like you was here yesterday. He was taking photographs.'

It is reasonable therefore to assume that when she set foot on this earth, head first, in the early hours of 1 August 1932,[1] courtesy a Master Ali Bux and Iqbal Begum, my heroine had small reason to rejoice at her birth. Iqbal Begum delivered her in the maternity ward of Dr Gadre's hospital in Parel, and when she was removed to her home in Dadar seven days later, there was no golden spoon in her mouth. Besides the spoon, she also, understandably, had no comprehension of the character of the world she had just arrived in; and although some of the events taking place around her were scarcely calculated to have

----

1   The date is confirmed but not the year. Some people say she was born in 1933.

any major influence on her life, I thought it would not be fully wasteful to evoke the feel and flavour of the times, and more specifically of the year, of her birth. What the historians like to call as 'placing in social context'.

The year 1932 has been variously described. Some called it the year of hope, others the year of peace, and still others the year of abandon. The ravages and the scars of a brutal war (1914–18) had just about healed and a whole generation of people began learning anew the forgotten art of enjoyment. It was also the year in which the pursuit of pleasure and leisure became respectable. 'Let's have a good time' was the prevailing philosophy of the day—and a mighty popular one.

In America, Herbert Hoover, the incumbent president, was campaigning vigorously for re-election—an election he was to lose to Roosevelt while Richard Nixon was still a student at law school. Norman Mailer, aged nine, sprouted his first obscenity when he heard his mentor Ernest Hemingway had successfully completed his only experimental novel *Death in the Afternoon* and J. Edgar Hoover moved in to smash the biggest kidnapping case of the year. In Hollywood, the Griffith era had come to an end (he made his last film in 1931) and two distinct new phenomena were gaining ground: one the Bogart–Cagney screen gangsters; the other W.C. Fields with his pitiless, mean, malicious, merciless brand of humour (in a film called *International House* he ordered the following Chinese meal: 'A couple of hundred-year-old eggs boiled in perfume'). Between these two, a third was trying to make its way—Charles Chaplin, a fumbling, bungling, losing little man formidably armed with bowler hat, walking stick and enough genius to sustain a generation. There is no elaborate evidence for this, but it is stated that the first-ever maxi skirt was worn by a preacher's daughter from Rapid City (South Dakota) in the year under surveillance.

In God's own country, Ramsay Macdonald was dutifully serving his monarch George V, King of Britain, Emperor of its Colonies and Defender of the Faith. Denis Compton scored his first century in first-class cricket and England lost the Ashes. The Nobel Prize for literature was bestowed on John Galsworthy while Noel Coward and Charles Laughton were the hottest new names on the stage and cinema. George Bernard Shaw, ageing though agile, decided that 'Beauty is all very well, but who ever looks at it when it has been in the house three days.' Ice cream in a cone made its debut on Brighton Pier and it took precisely thirty minutes for the first consignment to sell out.

On the Continent, Maurice Chevalier and Marlene Dietrich were fast establishing themselves as box-office stars, and somewhere gathering strength from the beer cellars of Bavaria another star called Hitler was emerging. The world's greatest painter, Picasso, was five years away from *Guernica*, and Fritz Lang had released his celebrated murder film *M*. Across the Urals, Stalin was rounding off his rivals. The Japanese conquered Manchuria and set up a puppet regime.

At home, Lord Irwin was viceroy and there seemed no immediate reason to hope that 'Swaraj' was near at hand. Nehru, now a recognized Congress leader, was mourning the death of his father, while Gandhiji and Sardar Patel were arrested and interned in Yervada Jail. Singing stars Saigal and Kanan Bala were the darlings of the audiences and Prithviraj had starred in India's first talkie. You could get nicely drunk for 84 paise (a bottle of beer costing 28), buy a kilo of sugar for 3 paise, smoke a packet of Gold Flake cigarettes for 10 paise, get a woollen suit stitched for Rs 3, find a decent whore for Rs 4. This then was the scenario.

Father Ali Bux, a Sunni Mosalman, was born in one of Mr Bhutto's villages in Pakistan called Bhera. Here he grew up to manhood, and from an early age took a deep and abiding interest in music. Additionally, he showed leanings towards writing in Urdu but didn't get very far in this direction. Ali Bux's musical career began with playing the harmonium on which he composed tunes and rendered them free for the benefit of his friends. In his village he became something of a celebrity and people called him Master Ali Bux. His parents married him off to a girl from his native place from whom he produced three daughters (one of these called Shama was later to play an important part in my heroine's life).

An astute man was Ali Bux. He soon realized that the outer reaches of the Punjab were hardly ideal for a budding, advancing musician. Carefully calculating the pros and cons he decided that his best prospects lay in the big city where a man of talent could find sustenance. In 1924, Ali Bux left his wife and daughters behind and emigrated to Bombay with not too much money but a lot of hope.

Unlike many he was fortunate and soon found employment. His were the days of the silent cinema and the stage, and he found work in theatres where, ingeniously hidden, he played his favourite harmonium. The move to Bombay had been profitable and there was more to come.

One of Ali Bux's working places was Krishna Company in Dadar and here, as he played his music, he set his eyes upon a slim, aristocratic Bengali Christian dancer named Prabhavati. To his music she moved her elegant body and very soon Ali Bux found it difficult to keep his mind on his harmonium.

The Bengali Christian danseuse came from Calcutta. She, besides being transparently lovely, was connected with the Tagore family. (Prabhavati's mother was the daughter of the poet's younger brother. She became a widow at an early age, embraced Christianity and left for Meerut. Here she married a gentleman called Pyare Lal and had two daughters. One of these was Prabhavati.) My heroine herself confessed that she remembered her mother, 'as a very beautiful woman'. Further, this beautiful woman was famous both as a heroine of the silent cinema and as a dancer on the stage. Love overflowing in his heart, Ali Bux proposed marriage to his danseuse with just one condition. She would have to renounce her religion. She agreed and Ali Bux found himself a second wife whom he called Iqbal Begum.

Seeing Ali Bux's picture one finds it difficult to understand how the beautiful, sensitive and talented Bengali dancer fell for him. By all accounts he was a stern, strict, God-fearing, humourless man. Given to wearing sherwanis and flapper pyjamas he seldom smiled or looked cheerful. Maybe it was his music that drew Iqbal to him.

One must remember that life in the 1920s for the professional stage and cinema artistes was precarious. There was firstly the social stigma of belonging to a vulgar trade and secondly salaries were low and irregular. So, although Ali Bux and wife in their respective spheres enjoyed a measure of popularity and success, they never made any substantial sums of money.

Ali Bux (affectionately known to all as 'Babujee') fathered three daughters in the order Khursheed, Mahajabeen and Madhu. This was a great disappointment to him because he desperately wanted a son. This disappointment was most pronounced when the second daughter was born and neighbours told a dejected Ali Bux that children irrespective of colour, sex and shape were the gift of Allah, and should be accepted as such. This made sense to him.

When it came to a name for my heroine there was no problem. Even when she was a few days old her moonlike face was shining brightly. They called her 'Mahajabeen', and it was a name that everyone thought to be highly appropriate.

By this time Ali Bux's eldest daughter Khursheed had established herself as a child star and her income supplemented the budget in the Bux household. Living was not extravagant but just about passable.

The year 1935 was one in which troubles began. Ali Bux contracted a strange debilitating illness which none of the local doctors seemed able to diagnose. Someone suggested that Babujee should go to Lahore for rest and treatment. This sounded like good advice and the entire family left for the Punjab. A three-year-old Mahajabeen (they used to call her 'Munna' at home) made her first railway journey not without incident. The train was passing over a bridge and the little girl feared that it would collapse. She closed her eyes and frantically tried to pull down the window, and in the process got her hand stuck in between and she fainted. When she opened her eyes a quarter of an hour later, she asked only one question: 'Have we crossed the bridge?'

Babujee improved steadily though unspectacularly and it took nearly a year for him to come back to Bombay. Whatever little savings he had were thus consumed in that year of sickness, and it was an impecunious Ali Bux who arrived back in Bombay to face the world.

Troubles come in pairs. Just as Iqbal was finding her feet back on the stage she began keeping indifferent health. After a prolonged and complicated examination it was confirmed that she had picked up an infection of the lung. Iqbal was determined to work but another incident happened which shattered her. Arrangements were being made at this time for the eldest daughter's marriage. While the delicate negotiations were in progress, someone from the bridegroom's side declared that the match was ill-fitting. 'The girl may be beautiful but she is still an actress's daughter.' This remark hurt Iqbal so much that she decided to give up her career for the sake of her daughters.

My own view is that the major reason for Iqbal's premature retirement was her health rather than her sensitivity to bitchy remarks. If she'd had a sound lung I am sure she would have continued her vocation.

With Iqbal out of the running and frequently bedridden, Ali Bux took on the job of nurse, mother and man about the house. Khursheed still managed to bring in small amounts from the various studios, but that was not enough, and father decided that there was nothing wrong in his two other girls earning their own keep.

As a parent he had very definite views on how to bring up his daughters. He frowned on any indulgence in sports—indoor or outdoor—which he considered a complete waste of time. Education too was something he had no great faith in and he believed that the bare minimum was essential. In accordance with these attitudes he wasted neither time nor money on his children in respect of textbooks or ping-pong racquets.

I suppose I am guilty of painting a picture of Ali Bux as a pretty heartless man. It was a picture which was confirmed by all who knew him or saw him. In fact there was never any great emotional attachment between the daughters and father. It was Iqbal who gave them love and understanding. Homi Wadia, with whom all the sisters worked, noticed this too. He observed that when the daughters were escorted to his studio by the father the atmosphere was always tense. However, when Iqbal accompanied the girls the atmosphere was more relaxed.

As a young girl, Mahajabeen frolicked and played around with other children of the neighbourhood in the vicinity of the many houses on her street. She was especially curious about one—the Rooptara Studio opposite her home. She saw so many cars go in and out that she assumed it must be an important place.

One day she plucked up courage and attempted to assuage her curiosity. But she was halted by a tall, big-moustached Pathan who watched over the entrance. He shooed her away and obediently she went to a shop adjacent which sold 'Garma Garam Pakoris'. She bought some, returned, and offered them to the forbidding Pathan. He knew he was being bribed but he accepted the offering, lifted the girl, planted a kiss on her mischievous face and took her personally inside the studio.

Further 'Pakoris' were not necessary since relations between Mahajabeen and the Pathan reached new accord. He would look the other way when this special girl ran into the studio.

There wasn't much time to play around though. Father commenced leading his four-year-old daughter to the various workhouses of Bombay. Respectfully he would call on the producers who were studio landlords too, and request, 'Sir, this is a very talented child. You must often be needing child artistes. Kindly do not forget this child, sir. It would be very kind of you.'

The hawking met with success. Vijay Bhatt, director,

producer and proprietor of Prakash Studios, heard Ali Bux
recite the same tale and he told him to bring his daughter to
work the next morning. He was then making *Leather Face* in
which Jairaj was the hero and Mehtab the heroine. There was
a vacancy for a small girl to play Jairaj's daughter, and this was
the part Vijay Bhatt had in mind for Mahajabeen.

Ali Bux woke his second daughter early the following day
and dressed her in her neatest frock. He chaperoned her to
Prakash Studios where Mahajabeen took to work like a fish
takes to water. She was neither intimidated nor overawed by
the surroundings or the equipment. Vijay Bhatt was quick to
spot this and secretly decided that if he ever needed a child
star again he would pick this very girl.

The shooting session over, it was payment time for the
extras. A huge and fabulous sum of 25 rupees was Mahajabeen's
share who could hardly believe this munificence.

From that day onwards there was no looking back. Film
followed film and in four years this funny-looking girl had
starred in *Adhuri Kahani, Pooja, Nai Roshni, Behan, Vijaya, Kasauti*
and *Garib.* Most of these were made by Vijay Bhatt and nearly
each morning she would go to his office in Parel from where
she was collected and taken in the producer's car to the studio
in Andheri. Meanwhile her salary had gone up which pleased
Ali Bux no end and eased the financial plight of the family.
(In an interview in 1962 she explained that the fact she had
been supporting her parents from the age of four gave her
immense satisfaction.)

How did she react to those early years? She herself states her
feeling eloquently. 'The first day I trotted along to work I little
imagined that I was saying goodbye to the normal pleasantries
of childhood. I thought I would go to the studio for a few days

and then go to school, learn a few things and play and make merry like other children. But that was not to be.'

Actually she was admitted into a regular school but that was not for long because the demands of work frequently interrupted her curriculum. She never went to school in any meaningful sense and her education was the result of private tuition and more significantly the result of individual interest. In every sense she was self-educated. (She concentrated most on Urdu although she could get by in English and Hindi.)

Mahajabeen had few childhood friends. All the friends she had were made in the studios. Cuckoo, who later became a famous dancing star, and Suresh, who became a hero and whom she described as 'shy and shabbily dressed', were her chief companions. She also became acquainted with one Baby Mumtaz who later made a name for herself as Madhubala.

Although she was completely at ease in the unreal neon-lit world of the studios, she didn't quite understand it. She thought it to be real rather than make-believe. During the shooting of *Leather Face,* she was informed that Jairaj was her father. She looked enquiringly at Ali Bux when she was told this and wondered how Jairaj could be her father when she already had one. In a fitting and poetic reversal fourteen years later, in *Magroor,* she became her make-believe father's lover. Of course by then she knew what the game was all about.

In front of the camera she always felt the absence of what all other children take for granted: a home life. As she confessed, 'It made me behave queerly as I now realize. I remember once I was "shot" on the sets and asked to drop down dead. I refused to fall and they had to use force to make me obey. I often played "back" for other children but refused to sing myself. My one interest was to read and when other children in the studio went out to play in the compound, I moved into a corner and lost myself in the world of children's books.' Observers were quick to notice this eccentricity and they nicknamed her 'Reading Mahajabeen'.

The year 1938 found Mahajabeen six years old and mini-famous. An up-and-coming writer called Kamal Amrohi was in quest of a seven-year-old girl to play a minor part in Sohrab Modi's *Jailor*. He was told to go and meet a Master Ali Bux in Dadar who had not one but three daughters, all talented, experienced and available.

Amrohi repaired to Dadar where Ali Bux greeted him with embarrassing courtesy and respect. The nature of the call established, Ali Bux sent for his daughters and one came running immediately, barefoot, with traces of mashed banana all over her face. Ali Bux apologized for the uncouth appearance of his daughter and said that she really looked quite nice without the fruit. Amrohi agreed and promised he would recommend the girl to Mr Modi.

As it turned out, Mahajabeen (was it because of the banana?) was not selected. However, one must record that these were the circumstances under which Mr Amrohi first set eyes upon the woman who was to haunt him for many years.

Meanwhile, Mahajabeen continued to work for Prakash Studios. On the sets of *Ek Hi Phool*, Vijay Bhatt concluded that Mahajabeen, as a name, was terribly unsuitable for a girl who was destined to go places. And it was he who suggested that Mahajabeen be called 'Baby Meena' instead. Ali Bux, who was beholden to Mr Bhatt, was not entirely happy with this arbitrary name-changing, but he was in no position to contest with the owner of Prakash Studios. So Baby Meena it was.

Why did they not call her just Meena? Why Baby Meena?

There is no answer for this except that every star who had
the indignity of travelling up from a tender age had the prefix
Baby mechanically fixed before his or her name. I think it
became an unquestioned practice and no one seriously disputed
it. Mahajabeen undoubtedly was a terrible name. Rigidly
Muslim (in a predominantly Hindu cinema) and unusually
uncommercial, it would have proved an albatross round my
heroine, and one must be grateful to Mr Bhatt for, if nothing
else, improving on it.

Purely on a personal level though, I find my heroine's film
name nondescript, sterile and flavourless. If she was going to
have a Hindu nom de plume she deserved something better.
I think we could all spend an intriguing evening finding
substitutes for Meena Kumari.

Child artistes have a habit of fading away. The very title
is destructive because you can't be a child artiste all your life.
As you grow older you automatically become disqualified.
Baby Meena in 1946, fourteen years old, faced her first big
test. The little girl's days were over and now only her real
ability could see her through. Opportunity came and she was
signed on opposite Agha in Ramnik Productions' *Bachchon Ka
Khel. Bachchon Ka Khel* turned out to be an ordinary film but
Baby Meena performed with credit and she was noticed at
this time by two other important film-makers, Kidar Sharma
and Homi Wadia.

Kidar Sharma was a director in Ranjit Movietone and Iqbal
Begum had requested Mr Sharma to give her daughter a chance
and entrusted him with the task, as he puts it, 'Of grooming
Mahajabeen into an accomplished actress. Her family would
be indebted to me for such a favour.' The favour was a film
called *Dada Jee* co-starring Jagirdar and Altaf (later to marry

Khursheed, Meena's eldest sister). The film was successfully completed but the negatives were destroyed in a fire.

I did not meet Mr Sharma but he is the exception when he says, 'She was rather dull and dumb-witted and at that time no one could predict that this girl would one day become the rarest on the Indian Screen.'

Contrastingly, Homi Wadia, the other film-maker she met at this time, told me, 'We could all see that this girl was going places. Everybody who came to the studio wanted to know who she was.'

With three girls working (Madhu had also started), fickle fortune began smiling on the Bux family. One of the first priorities was a new residence, and by the beginning of 1946 the Buxs were in a position to move and leave Dadar.

The house they procured was a neat little bungalow on Chapel Road, Bandra, next to Mehboob Studios, and it was blessed with a small garden, a small portico and many creepers. It was no Hilton but it was infinitely better than the 'Chawl'. You have only to go and see my heroine's first home to appreciate why she must have been overjoyed at the prospect of living in Bandra.

All three girls laughed and played in the garden, and Meena in particular took a fancy to plants and flowers and spent her spare time pottering around the garden. This interest in flora and fauna remained with my heroine till her very last.

Bux's attitude towards his daughters continued to be stern and businesslike. The wife suggested that he should get life insurance for his daughters. 'Why', he asked, 'do you think something is going to happen to them?' Actually he believed that if you took out an insurance policy you were somehow courting death.

He did not approve of my heroine's interest in the garden and thought it to be a colossal waste of time. In protest, she started throwing stones at the house next door. Here a young man called Naushad was at his wits' end trying to make some tunes. The unmelodious stone sounds finally compelled Naushad to complain to the master of the house next door. Babujee reprimanded my heroine with a slap. (Subsequently, in jest, Naushad would remind my heroine of the time he had got her beaten up.)

No one expected Iqbal to live very long. With her kind of affliction (lung cancer) it was just a matter of time. On 25 March 1947, after just eighteen months in the new house, Iqbal quietly passed away and was buried in the Sunni cemetery at Bandra. Ali Bux was now man and woman about the house.

Professionally, Meena was now securely in the hands of Homi Wadia and Basant Studios in Chembur. I went to meet Wadia one afternoon in Chembur. As I walked around a nearly desolate studio, I saw huge cut-outs and mud idols of our deities lying around. Homi Seth[2] (as he is popularly known), in case you did not know, is a celebrated maker of mythological and stunt films, and it was in the former type that work was mostly found for the young Meena Kumari.

The first film she made in Basant was called *Lakshmi Narayan* in which she played the goddess Lakshmi. She played this and subsequent goddess roles with such relish, religious fervour and conviction that one must wonder how she managed it. A Sunni Muslim girl, without even the rudimentary knowledge of Indian scriptures, conducted herself with such familiarity

---

2 Homi Seth's wife is stunt queen Nadia, and she also knew my heroine.

that people on the sets often mistook her for a Hindu girl. She was so perfect in these mythologicals that the early Meena became an essential feature of this genre.

The public noticed this too and after watching *Hanuman Patal Vijay*, *Shri Ganesh Mahima*, a Mr Malviya wrote an indignant letter to a film magazine asking the obvious question, 'If Meena Kumari is not a Hindu why is she always playing roles of Hindu goddesses?'

Just let's pause for a minute and consider the nature of mythologicals. They do, I think, purvey and dispense the most clear-cut, elementary and uncomplicated notions of morality. Good vs Evil is the heart of the theme and Good prevails. I am sure my heroine, after having personified Good in half a score of such films, emerged with a sense of virtue and rectitude which she must later have found to be oversimplified, if not false.

On the other hand there was money. She was paid Rs 4,000 for her first film and Rs 10,000 for her last (*Aladdin and the Lamp* with Mahipal which turned out to be a great hit) with Wadia. It was such moneys that enabled the family to buy the next status symbol, a second-hand Plymouth in 1950.

My heroine learned to drive immediately and became a passionate motor driver. Whenever she had the opportunity she would manoeuvre the rickety old Plymouth around the streets of Bandra.

Meena was now eighteen and no longer 'Baby Meena'. She became conscious of her body, her feminism and her sex. Reading an English monthly she fell upon a picture of a man. She stopped at that page. Something in the picture disturbed her. She looked under and discovered that it belonged to one Kamal Amrohi. It was a name she had overheard in many conversations in the studios. One and all spoke glowingly of this young writer-director who had recently scored a run-away success with *Mahal*. Reportedly, he had been paid a lakh of rupees for writing and directing this film. In the wake of *Mahal* in 1950, Kamal Amrohi was the hottest commodity around and many producers were keen to buy the services of this undisputedly talented though obstinate man: he knew exactly what he wanted from his film and was not inclined to make any compromises. (A trait that Mr Amrohi has been faithful to all his life.)

However, it was not the film-maker that aroused my heroine's curiosity. What set her heart beating was the writer, the man. Consistent with girls of her age, Meena was a romantic dreamer. In her mind's eye she had a clear picture of the person who was going to win her heart. He had to be clever. He had to be intelligent. He had to be a poet. He had to be a writer. The physical appearance of the man was of no consequence if he owned an engaging and scintillating mind.

Gazing at Mr Amrohi's photograph my heroine had 'lightning flash before my eyes, bringing realization with stunning shock which left me trembling, sick with a strange apprehension. This was the man of my dreams, the ideal enshrined in my heart. I did not want to believe it. I refused to entertain the thought. I tried to deceive myself. The vague figure I had cherished in my thoughts, hasty shadows of my dreams had suddenly taken on the shape and substance of an individual human creature. It couldn't be, I kept telling myself. But always there was a voice which seemed to say, "Do not be afraid to recognize me. I am really your ideal, not just a figment of your imagination." And finally I gave up and believed in that voice.' How she must have longed to meet him! (She had obviously forgotten the first encounter in Dadar twelve years ago.)

The summons of love were quickly answered. My heroine was working in a film with Dev Anand and Ashok Kumar called *Tamasha* and who should arrive at the sets but Kamal Amrohi and his friend/secretary Mr Baqar. Ashok Kumar performed the introductions and Mr Amrohi barely glanced at his future wife. 'He is a proud man,' thought my heroine and Ashok Kumar was a bit nonplussed too. He had expected the director to show more concern. After all he had introduced her to him with generous praise.

Mr Kumar offered, in a projection room upstairs, to show Amrohi the early rushes of *Tamasha* in order to convince him that what he had just neglected was no ordinary girl. Mr Amrohi, a reticent man, sat through the rushes in silence. However, on his way back home to Sion in the car he confided in Baqar, 'We must keep an eye on that girl.'

Kamal was employed then in casting for his next film *Anarkali*. A gentleman called Makhanlaljee was the producer and they had both agreed to use Madhubala and Kamal Kapoor in the title roles. Madhubala was approached and she seemed amenable. All was set for the next Amrohi venture.

A week later at 8 p.m., Kamal Amrohi was just about to sit down for dinner when the telephone rang. Makhanlaljee was on the other end.

'I have some bad news for you, Kamal.'

'You mean Madhubala has refused to star in *Anarkali*?'

'How did you know?'

'Well, at this moment I can't think of any other news which would be bad for me.'

Mr Amrohi told Makhanlal that all was not lost with the refusal of Madhubala and he would have a substitute heroine present at his house at ten in the morning, one who was equal

if not better than the one they had lost. (A minor reason for
Madhubala's refusal was that she insisted Dilip Kumar—with
whom she was allegedly having some kind of romance—be
hired instead of Kamal Kapoor. The major reason was Ataullah
Khan, Madhubala's father, who never had much faith in
Mr Amrohi as a film-maker.)

At 9.30 that night Baqar was entrusted with the task of
approaching Ali Bux at Bandra with a view to ascertaining
whether his second daughter was available for the role of
heroine in *Anarkali*.

At his residence in Bandra, Ali Bux was resting after dinner
on the ground of his garden when Baqar put the proposition.
Ali Bux could hardly contain himself. He stood up. It was his
honour and great good fortune, he said, that someone like
Kamal Amrohi had considered his daughter. He accepted
wholeheartedly and without reservations. My heroine, dressed
in a faint-blue garara kameez, heard this conversation blushing
from ear to ear. Her ideal man had slightly succumbed.

Baqar suggested that he come and pick the family up the
next morning for the meeting arranged with Makhanlaljee,
where the terms and conditions would be finalized. Bux said
there was no need for this since 'Aap Ki Dua Seh' (with your
blessings) he had his own car and would arrive at Makhanlaljee's
place unaided.

The meeting took place the next morning but Makhanlal
was not too hot on Meena. He couldn't believe that this untried
girl could undertake the role of *Anarkali*. Makhanlal took Ali
Bux to one side and offered Rs 3,000 for his daughter. He was
rightly offended at this ridiculous price and complained to Mr
Amrohi that the producer was indulging in a bit of horseplay.
Surely he didn't hope to secure a leading lady for that kind of

price? The haggling began and finally the figure of Rs 15,000 was in the air.

My heroine, in no way privy to these dealings, was nevertheless infuriated, and after watching the fluctuating starting prices left in the family car parked down below. Amrohi told a disappointed Ali Bux to go home and pacify his daughter. He promised that the 15,000 figure would somehow be agreed.

And so it was. On 13 March 1951, Meena put her signature on the contract and a relieved Kamal Amrohi left for Agra and Delhi to do some research and location shooting.

In April of that same year my heroine was stricken with an attack of typhoid. (She had never been a particularly healthy child and was frequently in and out of bed.) Three weeks later the temperature had subsided but the girl was pale and weak. The doctor recommended a change of air and the family decided to spend a couple of weeks in Mahabaleshwar—a hill station nearly 200 miles south of Bombay.

Meanwhile, Amrohi was busy in Agra and Delhi. The last few weeks had been uncommonly hectic and on 21 May his unit was resting in Cecil Hotel, Delhi. Just before dark a messenger arrived conveying the news that a film star called Meena Kumari had been involved in a motor accident while returning from Mahabaleshwar to Bombay. Mr Amrohi pressed for details but the messenger said he knew nothing beyond that.

The accident in fact was fairly serious. Meena, admitted in Sassoon Hospital, Poona, was severely damaged around the hand and there was some doubt whether she would be able to use it again. Ali Bux had three bones broken and wound up in plaster. Only Madhu got off lightly with minor injuries. The doctors confirmed that my heroine was in no mortal danger but they were not sure how long it would take for her to stand up again.

Lying in her hospital bed, Meena was going through terrible bouts of depression. She imagined her promising career lay in ruins and with it went the opportunity to work under the man she so dearly loved. 'My thoughts were at their saddest and my feelings at their lowest ebb one especially lonely evening when I lay wondering at my fate and what my future was to be.' That evening was 24 May 1951 and as she lifted her despairful eyes she saw standing near her bed the unmistakable figure of Kamal Amrohi. Mr Amrohi softly asked after my heroine's health but such was her joy that she was unable to answer. 'I was in a heaven of my own, uncaring of what was said or done, content merely to look and to know that Kamal was there, that he whom I had longed with such yearning had come to see me.'

Love began with a glass of 'Mosambi Juice'. The first day Amrohi arrived at the hospital it was nearly dusk. Sassoon was bathed in sensuous semi-darkness. Itinerant birds in the sky were making their way home. The air was sweet. Through an open window in Meena's room the last dying, flickering rays of the sun were quietly receding. Kamal was entranced by the poetry of the scene, and when my heroine's younger sister complained that 'appa' was not drinking her prescribed juice, he took the glass in his own hands, lifted Meena's head from the bed and placed the juice near her mouth. She drank it in one gulp. 'I just got caught in that glass,' Amrohi told me.

If you are looking for landmarks in my heroine's life, make a note of Sassoon Hospital, Poona, for it was here that Kamal and Meena really came together. Religiously once a week,

Mr Amrohi would drive down from Sion (the place where he lived in Bombay) to Poona and spend long hours nursing, encouraging and loving my heroine. Previously, Meena had known only the director, now once a week she got to know the human being and discovered in him areas of gentleness, humanity and loyalty. Previously, Kamal had known only the potential actress, now he got to know the woman, and discovered in her areas of scholarship, sensibility and sense. They seemed then, to borrow the current advertising slogan, 'Made for each other'.

Once a week clearly was not enough. And the lovers found an answer to that too. When they were not scheduled to meet, both my heroine and Mr Amrohi would write letters: one letter per day. However, no stamp was affixed; on the day of the visit they were exchanged in person.

Close your eyes for a minute and imagine. A car enters a hospital and a thirty-one-year-old man wearing a black sherwani gets out and walks towards a private room. There a girl of eighteen is restless on her bed, sometimes looking at the clock, sometimes at the calendar, sometimes at the door. At last it opens and the man she is expecting walks in. Both smile and beyond that nothing happens except the exchange of two packets. In one packet are the letters written by the man to the woman, in the other are the letters written by the woman to the man. The room has a balcony and the man and his packet advance in that direction. He leans against one of the walls and begins reading his accumulated mail. Sitting on the bed the girl does likewise. The reading over, the man comes and sits by his woman. Nothing more needs to be said. They just look.

On one such visit my heroine decided that Kamal was decidedly too formal a name for a lover. Mr Amrohi agreed and said that when he was young, and even now, the elders in his house called him 'Chandan'. She grabbed at that. Not to be left behind, Mr Amrohi expressed distaste for the title Meena Kumari. It was too filmi, too public. 'Would you mind if I called you Manjooh?' (The middle one—Meena being the middle girl in her family.) 'No,' replied my heroine, 'but could you possibly make it Manju, it's so much better than Manjooh.' No arguments, the christening was complete.

On another night a declaration of love was inscribed on the forearm. My heroine asked the director if despite her accident she was still in the running for *Anarkali*. There was no question, he said, of her being out. Then he took a pen and etched on her hand the word *Anarkali*. Had he left it at that this artistry would have been prosaic and unexceptional. But he didn't. What he did was to put alongside 'Meri' (Mine).

The person whose hand had been scribbled read this autograph, placed the writing on her forehead, and sighed.

One could conclude from all this that both my heroine and Mr Amrohi had a special weakness for symbols. However, don't you think in this instant and desensitized age, where sentiment is a dirty word, these two romantics have a lesson for us all?

Sometimes Amrohi was delayed in Bombay and failed to keep his once-a-week schedule. When this happened there would be a call from Poona to Bombay Talkies that a certain patient was refusing to take her medicines or her food. She said she would accept these only from the hands of a Mr Amrohi. Could they send him up quickly?

For four months this hospital affair continued and each month it grew in passion and intensity. Finally my heroine was pronounced fit with a damaged hand—a hand that remained damaged all her life—and she hated getting well. Now where was she to meet her lover? Allah! Could she have another accident.

Shooting on *Anarkali* began as soon as Meena got back to Bombay and the first session was a jail scene which, according to those who have seen the rushes, should be kept in an institution. They say it is possibly the best historical few thousand feet in Indian cinema. My heroine was magnificent and Kamal Amrohi now had irrefutable evidence that the woman he loved was a fine actress.

And then the marathon and famous telephoning began. Mr Amrohi would dial my heroine's number from Sion at 11.30 in the night and replace the receiver at 5.30 in the morning. A confidant of Mr Amrohi who was privileged to hear this record-breaking tête-à-tête told me that not many words were spoken. Frequently, there would be long Pinterish pauses and then Amrohi would say, 'I forgot to tell you of an incident at the studio this afternoon ...' And after having related this incident there would be another long pause. And so on. My heroine at her end did not even have the receiver tuned into her ear. Instead, she placed it on her breast so that it was directly in contact with her heart.

How come the vigilant Ali Bux was ignorant about these nocturnal communications? The answer is simple. In Meena's house the telephone was next to her bedroom and when it rang at the stipulated hour she would whisk it away to her bedroom, secure the door, hide the instrument under her bedsheet and be reassured by her father's snoring sounds. (These telephone calls continued till Meena left her house two years later in favour of Kamal's and there is a view that these late-night exchanges contributed to my heroine and Mr Amrohi becoming firm insomniacs later on in life.)

Work on *Anarkali* did not get very far. Makhanlaljee, the producer, had a weakness for the stock market and as frequently happens, lost his 'dhoti'. He suffered a crippling financial disaster and Amrohi, who had ambitious plans for his film, wisely realized that he could not make a vivid and honest historical on a shoestring budget. Makhanlal sportingly offered the director his last paisa but alas that wasn't enough. *Anarkali* was abandoned in an atmosphere of recrimination and despondency. Many felt that Mr Amrohi should have cut his losses and made the best of a bad historical.

Such, by now, was my heroine's faith in Mr Amrohi that she took the cancellation without too much gloom—possibly because she had received two other important and interesting assignments, and one of these was later destined to launch her right into the big league. Zia Sarhadi sent her the script of *Footpath* and Vijay Bhatt of *Baiju Bawra*. Meena read these scripts and for expert opinion forwarded them to Kamal. Mr Amrohi was more taken up by Sarhadi than Bhatt's offering but recommended that my heroine accept both. It was a monumental recommendation because who knows where my heroine would have been without her *Baiju*.

THREE

Rise

Success is the necessary misfortune of life, but it is only to the very unfortunate that it comes early.

– Anthony Trollope

Love affairs have a tendency to spill—especially when the participants happen to be famous. In late 1951, the word was buzzing around inside the industry of the association of a beautiful actress and a mercurial film-maker. The gossip-mongers, however, were aware of problems. Mr Amrohi was nearly fifteen years my heroine's senior and, additionally, the possessor of one wife and three sons; and although the holy book granted four partners, a lot of people wondered whether Meena would happily accept the title of 'Chhoti Ammi' (smaller mother).

Surprisingly, the actual participants had never discussed the subject of marriage. They considered it privately in their own minds but never spoke aloud, and for the moment it was sufficient for them just to be fondly in love. It wasn't alas sufficient for those who were breathlessly waiting for the outcome of the flirtation.

Cupid was not my heroine's sole preoccupation these days. *Tamasha* was fast nearing completion and shooting dates for both *Footpath* and *Baiju Bawra* had been agreed. It must have been a rigorous routine: work in the morning, telephone calls at night—but then true love, we are told, is no respecter of time or energy.

Perhaps the one person who disapproved most strongly of the Kamal infatuation was Madhubala. It appears she had an old crush (from the time of *Mahal*) on him and was given to writing Kamal with chalk on every vacant place in Bombay Talkies studio. Mr Amrohi, I was told, gave Madhubala 'no lift' and it is not difficult to see why. Despite her very visible physical charms she had none of my heroine's intellectual and poetic qualities, and the maker of *Mahal* was not the kind of man who gave in to skin-deep beauty alone.

Madhubala stopped an Amrohi friend and asked him point-blank, 'Is it true what I hear about Meena and Kamal?' The friend replied yes, it was true. She asked no more.

Three days later, fairly late at night she drove into Bombay Talkies and found Kamal sitting with his friends sipping tea. She requested him to step outside for she had an urgent and personal matter to discuss with him. He stepped outside and forthwith Madhubala offered Mr Amrohi her hand in marriage and three lakhs of rupees. She said she would come and live with him as his wife; only he would have to send his three sons to Amroha (Kamal's native village in UP). Meena's future husband disdainfully refused this bargain with the comment, 'I only sell my stories; not my children.'

This curious proposal set Kamal seriously thinking. Either he would have to break up with my heroine or continue the affair to its logical and respectable end. He was too old and too old-fashioned for illicit love. What was he to do, he asked his friend Baqar, 'This woman (Meena) has got me under her spell.'

Baqar was quite clear that there was only one avenue open. If you truly love this woman, he said, take the step worthy of this love—marry her, bring her into your home, set her up as your lawfully wedded wife.

At her end in Bandra, Meena was not oblivious to the rumours and gossip circulating about her. But she was too proud to suggest anything like matrimony to the man who telephoned her each night. In her heart she was sure that when the right moment came he would ask for her.

Baqar was once again the emissary. He met my heroine and enquired plainly whether she loved his boss. 'I do. I do,' she replied. Then marry him and put a stop to this telephonic nonsense. Meena asked immediately, 'But what of Babujee. He will never agree to this match. How can I get married without his permission?'

Actually she did. At 8 p.m. on 14 February 1952, when Ali Bux drove his two daughters as usual to Dr Jussawala's clinic in Warden Road, he knew nothing of the plot hatched between Meena, Madhu, Kamal and Baqar. Ever since her accident, my heroine was a patient of this famous doctor who had a 'massage clinic', and who administered to her damaged hand. On this particular evening, as their father reversed his car and left, Madhu and Meena did not go up into the clinic (Ali Bux was in the habit of leaving his two girls and returning two hours later to pick them up); instead, they hopped into a waiting Buick.

The younger sister Madhu, precisely informed of this conspiracy, had been a source of great solace to my heroine and had encouraged her to take Kamal's hand. As the car drifted,

Madhu sat next to a nervous Meena, reassuring her that all would go well. Kazi Sahab had already been informed that his services would be required, and he was ready and waiting with his two sons when the Buick arrived.

Without much ado, Kazi Sahab began the simple 'Nikah' ceremony, first according to Sunni ritual, then according to Shia ritual. The 'Nikah' paper was witnessed by Baqar and the priests' two sons, and signed in the name of Mahajabeen and Sayeed Amir Hyder 'Kamal Amrohi'.

Marriage over, there was just time for a hasty kiss on the forehead, and then the newly-weds were parted. Mr Amrohi left for Sion, and Madhu and Meena returned to Warden Road to await their father's return. It was 9.45 when the sisters got to the clinic and they pretended to go up the stairs. At exactly ten they came down, waited for two minutes and sure enough Ali Bux drove up. Amrohi and Baqar, who were watching this from a distance, were now sure that the master plan had been perfectly executed.

When Ali Bux came he had no reasons to be suspicious. He gathered my heroine on time and as he drove her home he had not the slightest inkling that his second daughter was now alien property.

My heroine and Mr Amrohi had been entirely practical about their wedding. They decided to keep it a secret until such time Meena was able to present her father with a purse of Rs 2 lakh. She was painfully aware that if she abruptly left the family without providing for her aged father and younger sister (Khursheed had married and moved out to set up her own home in Pakistan) they would be in very uncomfortable straits indeed. Kamal was entirely sympathetic with this edifying sense of family responsibility and said he would bide his time until the required sum was collected, and in the mean time would visit his wife one day in a week (Sunday). Beyond that he extracted only one promise: the telephone conversations must continue.

By April of 1952, *Tamasha* was safely in the can and my heroine had commenced work on *Baiju Bawra* in right earnest. Most of the shooting took place in Prakash Studios with just a few stints of outdoor in a place called Aptanagar, 60 miles from Bombay. On days she wasn't required by Mr Bhatt, she reported to the director of *Footpath*, Zia Sarhadi. Bimal Roy, who was contemplating a Hindi version of a Bengali novel by Sarat Chandra Chatterjee, approached Meena tentatively regarding the main role. Bombay Talkies was interested in signing her on for one of their ventures, *Kohinoor*. There certainly seemed no shortage of work.

How the matrimony leaked to Ali Bux no one knows. Some say that he was informed by the house cook who had heard Meena on the telephone to Amrohi. Some say that Kazi Sahab was the carrier pigeon. Some say that sister Madhu inadvertently let out the news. Ali Bux, however, was wiser and confronted his daughter with the vital question. He demanded a straight answer. She confirmed his worst suspicions. He was furious. How could she, he asked, his own flesh and blood, deceive him in such a manner? She was so innocent, did she appreciate the enormity of what she had done? Did she pause to consider how disastrously inept a choice she had made? My heroine did not attempt to answer these charges. With tears in her eyes she left for her room and bolted the door.

When she met her husband next she told him that life was quite intolerable, with Ali Bux regularly hurling accusations, and recommending that it was still not too late. A divorce could be arranged, said Ali Bux, and he was more than willing to approach Amrohi in this connection. The husband counselled patience and told his wife to concentrate on work. They both hoped that as time passed Ali Bux would accept or at least become resigned to something which was now irrevocable. Before she left, she presented her husband with a copy of the Koran in which she had written, 'By the grace of Allah I am your lifelong, legally wedded wife. Even if you murder me, not a single sound or word of complaint will pass my lips.' There are some people I met who insist that there is more truth in these lines than meets the eye.

Fortunately, the pressure of work on my heroine was such that she did not have the time to argue with her father. *Baiju Bawra* and *Footpath* were now in full swing and nearly every night Meena returned home fairly late. After dinner she went straight for the telephone.

July 1952 found Meena waiting anxiously for the release of her first big film, *Tamasha*. Directed by Phani Mazumdar and co-starring Dev Anand and Ashok Kumar this film flopped at the ticket counter. It was not my heroine who was incompetent, but the film. Suggested as a parody on the Indian film industry this offering was as precocious as unimaginative. Some of the blame for this film rubbed off on my heroine. A press review of *Tamasha* pronounced, 'Meena Kumari disappoints. She is dull and unimpressive.' This was a review with which many agreed and the sceptics began questioning whether Baby Meena was going to make it.

Baiju Bawra once again brought my heroine near death. In August, Vijay Bhatt and unit were shooting the famous song *'Tu Ganga Ki Maoj Mein Jamuna Ka Dhara'* in Aptanagar. If you remember, the setting was Baiju calling after his Gauri who was vainly trying to avoid him (the hamlet lasses were teasing her because of her amours with the long-haired wayward singer). In order to avoid him she gets inside the local boat and rows midstream, unheeding Baiju's love call.

Ali Bux, who usually accompanied his daughter to work, had some forebodings about this scene. He turned his back to the shooting and as he looked the other way he remembered what a wise astrologer had told him many years ago: 'Keep your daughter away from fire and water. They could be very dangerous for her.' However, the family budget took precedence and required my heroine to go midstream, contrary to the warnings of the sage.

The water sequence was completed without disaster, but inside the boat my heroine had begun to enjoy herself. She was new to oars, rivers, boats, and when Mr Bhatt shouted 'cut' over the loudspeaker she pretended not to hear. Instead, she persevered in the opposite direction, tremendously enjoying the big open sky and the feel of the water below her. Further, the next shot was after lunch, so my heroine knew that there was no great urgency to return ashore.

In her stream travels she detected a slight acceleration in the speed of her boat. This excited her further and she was not in the least bothered by the four or five people waving and wildly gesticulating to her. In actuality they were warning her to return whence she came; she thought they were fans expressing regard. Little did she know that 100 yards ahead was a deep fatal fall in the stream and had she got her fragile boat involved in that whirlpool, she would have surely perished.

Suddenly, she discovered her boat to be unmanageable. The oars were useless against the strong current and she was being driven inexorably towards the fall whose gushing downward sound she could now hear distinctly. Helpless, she closed her eyes for she had not the courage to see her own death, which she felt sure was at hand. Inside the rocketing boat, she apologized to her father, said farewell to her husband and thought of the poor producer whose film would be ruined by this drowning. 'But I am dying. What can I do,' she ruminated.

Providence in the shape of a stone saved her. There were many fierce rocks in the stream and Meena's craft collided with one. Her boat miraculously stopped, and when she opened her eyes she noted that barely fifteen yards away was the fall.

Ali Bux, on land, was invoking all the gods he could think of and cursing himself for exposing his second and most precious daughter to forewarned hazards. When Meena finally came ashore unscathed he swore that from that day onwards the only water this daughter of his was going to see was under her shower.

The shooting for *Baiju Bawra* also revealed an interesting contradiction in my heroine. She was terrified by insects and particularly the hideous cockroaches, yet she showed a partiality to snakes. Mr Bhatt's plot required that Gauri physically sacrifice herself so that Baiju could get on with the job of seeking his vengeance with Tansen. Bravely she holds out her hand towards a venomous snake, requesting him to do the needful. As soon as this picturization was complete (a non-venomous snake had been especially procured), my heroine casually caught hold of the reptile and started stroking it. Everyone present on the set was amazed. 'Aren't you afraid,' someone asked. She said no, and continued playing with her friend.

Around now, husband and wife had their first tiff. Kamal, troubled that life for his wife had become impossible at home due to the insults of family and relatives, suggested to Meena in a letter that they could still possibly reconsider the step they had taken in the mosque. My heroine in reading this letter felt that Mr Amrohi underestimated the strength and sincerity of her feeling, and sent back a biting reply, 'My opinion is that you will not be able to understand me, and I will not be able to understand you. It would be better for you to divorce me.' Mr Amrohi claims that he replied punctually, saying that if she so desired, he would, whenever she wished, take her to Kazi Sahab and unbind from earlier vows.

My heroine kept this letter and did not pursue the matter of separation any further. Very soon the motion picture of her life was to be released and she was basking in the advance publicity. *Filmfare*, at that time the most prestigious film magazine, published a profile and remarked, 'She has an exciting photogenic face—the sort that cosmetic manufacturers dream of ... she finds herself with two much talked about and significant films, *Footpath* and *Baiju Bawra*, and more contracts are pouring in each week.'

True they were, but my heroine was anxiously waiting for the reception of *Baiju Bawra*. She could hardly forget that her last film, *Tamasha*, had not done much for her and a second failure would probably have sealed her fate. One lapse is forgivable, two lapses and you are out.

Baiju Bawra was released on 5 October 1952 in Bombay and the reviews were ecstatic: 'Considering the success of other stars in the course of the year, it can be easily said that the promising new star (Meena) will be ranked among the first five stars of the year on the merit of her outstanding acting in *Baiju Bawra*.' The entire film press corps was unanimous in its praise. A brand-new star had been sighted.

Vijay Bhatt's film was no ordinary hit. It was a gigantic, enormous, record-breaking hit. I have done no research on this, but I suspect that in the hierarchy of box-office successes in Indian cinema *Baiju Bawra* must rank very high indeed. It ran for 100 weeks in Bombay and completed silver, golden and diamond jubilees all over India.

What was the secret of *Baiju Bawra*'s success? It was not a very intelligent, very provocative, very authentic period film. The histrionics of both Bharat Bhushan and my heroine were in no way outstanding. The handling of the historical material showed little understanding or respect for the past. The central theme was time and time again marred by unnecessary deviations of plot. So whose success?

Unquestionably two individuals: Naushad and Rafi. These two men, the music director and playback singer, were solely responsible for all the diamond jubilees.

The public loved it. They saw it not once, not twice, but fifteen, sixteen times and came out humming, '*Ab To Nir Baha De*', '*Man Tarpat Hari Darshan Ko*'. I was young, just eleven years old, but I remember a family acquaintance who was much in demand at our parties because everyone said he was a 'second Mohd. Rafi'. Late at night my father along with others would urge him to sing *Baiju Bawra* songs. After some 'nakhra' he would oblige, and all the invitees would close their eyes and melodiously shake their heads as he sang.

If my heroine was unlucky with *Tamasha*, she was exceedingly lucky with *Baiju Bawra*. I went to see this film recently in Chinchpokli and found her performance not noteworthy. She was neither good nor bad. The script expected of her that classic peasant belle routine. Simple and innocent, she went through the motions with no special excellence. However, the moneymakers were immediate to notice that a man called Vijay Bhatt had made a lot of money with a film star called Meena Kumari. Unless she did something stupendously stupid she was secure for a few years as far as signing contracts was concerned. You can in Bombay fool some of the people some of the time.

Among the many people who congratulated my heroine for her fine performance was Kamal Amrohi. The telephone calls and Sunday visits had stopped in between and this congratulatory excuse enabled both Kamal and Meena to bury the hatchet. He said she was terrific as Gauri, and she said she was glad to hear his voice again. Mr Amrohi informed his wife that he had not been idle in the past few months and had been working ferociously on a film script which he had just concluded. Naturally, the leading role in this was reserved for Meena, and she accepted it without even reading a line.

Here *Baiju Bawra* had just finished and there Mr Bimal Roy had performed the mahurat of *Parineeta*, in which my heroine landed the main part. But there was also two setbacks. Some of the negatives of Sarhadi's *Footpath* were destroyed in a fire, and Meena who had been angling for work in S.U. Sunny's *Udan Khatola* was told politely, no, thank you—the part was going to Nimmi.

As if these reverses were not enough, *Filmfare* on 31 October 1952 conducted a Beauty Poll with the seemingly impossible task of placing in order of priority the three most beautiful film women of India. The panel of selectors comprised actors, producers, directors, and they voted Nalini Jaywant No. 1, Nargis No. 2, and Madhubala No. 3. My heroine trailed a poor No. 8, and the selection, as far as I am concerned, shows how uninformed the panel was when it came to matters of beauty.

That my heroine was never a convincing and polished liar was also made evident at this juncture. A film mag organized a Rs 2,000 monthly crossword competition called 'Filmwords' and approached various stars for testimonials recommending this contest. Meena, conscious that it was important to maintain harmonious relations with the press, wrote this: 'For years I have been yearning for a competition dealing with films. I find "Filmwords" just the thing. I am agog over them.' If I know my heroine, she was anything but agog over something as unintelligent as a crossword puzzle.

These were days when Ali Bux was having a trying time keeping pace with dates and schedules for his daughter. She was so heavily in demand that he had to turn down many offers. However, on her behalf he had put his signatures on *Naulakha Haar*, *Dana Pani*, *Bank Manager*, *Ilzam* and *Amar*. There was only one film which he was ignorant about. This was Kamal Amrohi's *Daera* which his daughter had accepted, and which subsequently was instrumental in causing her to leave her father's house.

On 14 February 1953, with a nice sense of occasion (it was the first wedding anniversary), Meena telephoned Kamal from Khandala where she had gone for a weekend holiday. She told him she had torn his communication regarding divorce. He said he was glad she had done so. Thus the first tiff was officially patched up.

Acrimony, however, was waiting for my heroine when she came back from the mountains. She informed her father that she was required by her husband for his film. Ali Bux said this was impossible since he had already agreed with Mehboob Sahab that she would report every morning for the shooting of *Amar*. He refreshed her memory that Mehboob Sahab was not an ordinary film-maker, and as an actress her best prospects lay with him. Further, this film had Dilip Kumar as hero and she should know what that meant.

Reluctantly, Meena agreed to present herself before Mehboob Sahab, but precisely five days after attendance she instigated a disagreement with Mehboob and left the studios.

The following day my heroine disclosed to her father that she was off to Bombay Talkies where Amrohi was working on *Daera*. Ali Bux warned his daughter that if she went in that direction the doors of Bandra would be permanently shut for her.

Defiantly, on 14 August 1953, my heroine drove to Bombay Talkies and worked in front of her husband's camera. When she came back, her father, who by now had made enquiries and knew exactly where she had been, refused to open the door. Sister Madhu came outside and tried to dissuade her father but he was adamant. Meena, unapologetic, asked Madhu to fetch a dozen of her saris and when these were at hand she calmly turned her car and left for Mr Amrohi's residence at Sion.

When she arrived at Sion, Mr Amrohi was still not back from work, and the servant let her in. 'Where is the bedroom?' she asked this man. The servant dutifully led her to that room. Here she saw what she had been looking for—the wardrobe, and inside it she hung her saris and left.

Twenty minutes later she reappeared, and this time the master was in. He in fact had just returned, and while turning his latch key had heard his telephone ring. Anticipating Meena's call he rushed in only to discover it was a wrong number. He had hardly placed the receiver back when the person whose call he had been expecting came straight through the door.

'What are you doing here?' he asked, astonished. She beckoned him into the bedroom and indicated her hanging saris.

Mr Amrohi was overjoyed when he became conversant with the details. He told his wife not to worry. She was safe in his house.

That night at 10.30 my heroine wrote a letter to her father:

> Babujee, whatever has happened I have left. Please do not talk about going to court. That would be childish. I desire nothing from your house except my clothes and books. This car I now have I will send to you tomorrow. My clothes, etc., you can send when you find it convenient. Please reply by letter or through the phone.
>
>   Meena

Ali Bux received this letter and panicked. He made attempts to make up with his daughter but she resisted any overtures and made plain that she was determined to stay by her husband.

Despite these problems work continued uninterrupted and news of the marriage became public. The press commented: 'Meena Kumari's reputation as the quiet and silent girl of the Indian cinema was aided considerably by her announcement of her marriage which had been kept secret for over a year.'

A marriage sans honeymoon allowed my heroine to complete *Footpath, Parineeta, Daera, Dana Pani, Naulakha Haar* by November 1953. Patricia Pereira, a film journalist, enquired of my heroine how she managed to finish so many films in so short a time. 'I work from sunrise till midnight,' she replied.

There was another reason. Ever since she had moved in with Amrohi, he and his friend Baqar took over the job of negotiating contracts, collecting money and fixing shooting dates. They were so ruthlessly efficient in this task that Meena found no difficulty working in four or five films simultaneously. This efficiency continued till Meena left the Amrohi house, and the figures speak for themselves. In the eleven years they lived together Meena completed nearly fifty out of her seventy-seven films.

Looking back on 1953 my heroine had every reason to be satisfied. The marriage was going well and her cinema career was securely launched. Babujee had given up his mission to get his daughter back to Bandra, and the younger sister Madhu had found the man of her life—a Mr Mehmood (who we all know today simply as Mehmood). Things couldn't be better.

But the crowning accolade was still to come. At the fag end of 1953, Hindustan Lever, makers of Dalda and Lux toilet soap, secured my heroine as a model for their beauty soap. This was a much coveted honour and when the Lux advertisement appeared no one could deny its indication. Meena Kumari had arrived.

Kamal Amrohi's first wife naturally had not taken news of her husband's marriage lightly. She started getting periodic attacks of nervous fits and these became progressively worse. A few days before my heroine moved to Sion she was despatched to Kamal's native village Amroha, and here she subsequently spent a large portion of her life.

Just before Meena had left her father's house, a pretty-looking girl called Firdaus came to see her at the studios. She said she was destitute with nowhere to go. My heroine, generous to a fault, purchased her some new clothes, engaged her on a monthly salary as an ayah and commenced bringing her to work regularly. This woman didn't do much except stand around Meena decoratively. Baqar took Meena to one side and recommended that it would be better if she left this woman at home. The habits of the cinema people not being too high, she was exposing this girl to needless moral hazards. Meena agreed and as suggested left her at Bandra.

However, while Meena was at work, this Firdaus began pitching her charms at Ali Bux, a lonely old man now. Rumours started flying. A month after she left Bandra, Meena learned that her father had proposed marriage to this woman. She refused to countenance this ignominy and sent someone to fetch all her belongings from Ali Bux's house. It was a symbolic gesture but it indicated that the break now was total.

Possibly taking cue from her elder sister, Madhu eloped and married her lover Mehmood. They too began living together. Poor Ali Bux was left all alone.

The scene now shifts from Sion to Pali Hill. In the 1950s, this slightly elevated, undulating, piece of real estate was almost deserted. Today it is the Sunset Boulevard[1] of India. In every cottage, every skyscraper there is ensconced some personality of the film industry. So in a way the move from Sion to Pali Hill was movement in the affluent direction. The flat that Mr Amrohi had acquired was in a building called 'Rembrandt.' Muddy red in colour, this building has no lift and on the second floor is a white door inside which lived Mr and Mrs Kamal Amrohi for twelve years.

In Rembrandt my heroine spent possibly the two or three happiest years of her life. For her, Kamal had the wisdom of Socrates, the charm of Aly Khan, the intelligence of Indira Gandhi and the sex appeal of Rajesh Khanna. Husband and wife would while away their spare time lounging around,

---

1 Hollywood's Pali Hill.

looking at each other, playing 'rummy'[2] and generally talking and reading. Frequently, in Mr Amrohi's Buick they would go and see an English film. In every sense they behaved like a couple who considered even a moment's separation too much.

'I am in love, yes I am in love, with a married man, who is married to me,' she wrote and continued, 'more than a year has passed since I got married and I am still the happiest person in the world because the man I have married is still the ideal man I loved before I had ever met him. We understand each other completely. Kamal has lived up to my every thought of him. I hope, indeed I know, he will say the same of me. Something of the deep understanding and kinship of soul which is between us may perhaps be seen in the picture we have just made together, *Daera*.'

This is the undisguised authentic voice of a woman madly, passionately, crushingly in love. So when she says, 'There is between us a bond of love which transforms all human activity and invests its most prosaic manifestation with the beauty of art, makes poetry of ordinary actions of everyday life: like fetching your husband's slippers or merely reading the paper together,' she is not one bit exaggerating.

Out of a batch of six, only three 1953 films of Meena Kumari deserve comment: *Daera, Footpath* and *Parineeta*.

The first two were spectacular failures while the third did moderately at the box office. *Footpath*, made by the Marxist Sarhadi was almost Godardian in content. A noble and socially committed offering, it attempted to portray the degradation, poverty and despair experienced by Bombay's roadside dwellers. In this noble failure, my heroine, friends

---

2 My heroine's favourite card game.

and foes alike agreed, showed for the first time that in the hands of a sympathetic director and discriminating script, she was capable.

Daera served only to confirm this impression. Directed, produced and scripted by Amrohi, this film ran for two days in Bombay and that perhaps is a measure of its excellence. Based on a true life episode, *Daera* crystallized poignantly the repressed sexual energies of a young girl married to a dying old man. As a woman coming to terms with her thwarted physical passions, my heroine gave a hauntingly moving, yet restrained performance. Discerning critics noted this and commended, 'Meena Kumari is exquisite ... as delicate as a gossamer yet expressing emotion with the vivid power of life and the tragic strength of death. Her portrayal is a gem of histrionic art.'

Parineeta, commercially most successful out of this trio, was a shrewd Bimal Roy film. It combined in exactly the right proportion familiar box-office ingredients with penetrating social comment. The author of the novel, Sarat Chandra Chatterjee, conceived his story as a blow against the rigid class classification prevalent in sections of Bengali aristocracy; Bimal Roy turned this message into predominantly a love story.

It was my heroine, however, who held the shaky structure of this film together. As Lalita, the poor relative turned housegirl serving the young master (Ashok Kumar), she was at once candid, calculating and sweet.

Besides collecting money, Bimal Roy's film did two things for my heroine. One, it conclusively demonstrated that she was an actress of considerable and perhaps untapped talent. Two, it cemented one of the most popular romantic teams in Indian cinema: Ashok Kumar and Meena Kumari.

Romantic team is a phenomenon which has ancient

antecedents, and which prevails till today. Currently, Mr Rajesh Khanna and Miss Sharmila Tagore are inseparable in the public eye; similarly, in 1954, Dilip and Nimmi were inseparable. And so were Raj Kapoor and Nargis, Bharat Bhushan and Suraiya, and Meena Kumari and Ashok Kumar.

It appears they got on famously, and artistically really got to know each other during *Parineeta*. This was more of a woman's film and Mr Kumar was exceedingly chivalrous in not hogging the limelight. He stayed unobtrusively in the background and this forced my heroine to have a 'high regard for him'. She thought he was the best of them all, and all then included Dilip, Dev, Bharat and Nasir Khan.

Despite Mr Kumar's forty-two years, my heroine, twenty-two years his junior, found him to be compatible, coaching and comradely. 'He never puts on any airs, never tries to force his talent and experience on anybody. I have always found him to be helpful and cooperative, and whenever I do a scene wrong he makes me do it the right way not by saying "this is how it must be done", but "don't you think it would be better if it was done this way".' Like me, you are probably wondering where the director was when these lessons were going on.

Observe the Meena-Ashok team closely and you will notice that there is no immediate logic or appeal in the combination. Mr Kumar in 1954 was a big, robust individual with short, nicely oiled curly hair. Mostly, he would be seen smoking a cigarette and extinguishing it after a few perfunctory puffs. He also had a weakness for short, long-sleeves bush shirts which invariably had a scarf dangling down the neck (for trend watchers this dangling scarf was the sartorial symbol of the 1950s). My heroine on the other hand was a petite, delicate, fragile maiden, and together on the screen they looked more like father and daughter rather than two hot irresistible lovers.

But it would be futile to deny the pulling power and attraction of this team. How and why these two wonderful opposites came together is another mystery that the writer of this book will not attempt to unravel.

On Sunday, 21 March 1954, Metro cinema situated in Dhobi Talao was wearing its best. Cleaned, scrubbed and decked with colourful buntings it was the venue of the first Filmfare Awards.

Now *Filmfare* was a film magazine which came into existence in 1952 and ever since had become the most sensible mouthpiece of the Indian cinema industry. Pictorially gay and editorially incisive, it was in my opinion much more virile and pioneering in its early years than it is now. Then true to its spirit, *Filmfare* seized upon the excellent idea of instituting awards for various excellences connected with the cinema—a commendable idea and one which is in existence till today.

That my heroine was being actively canvassed for the 'Best Actress' award was common knowledge to all, and by the beginning of 1954 it was virtually in the bag. There were no other serious contenders in the running and the one or two who were being considered proved no match for Gauri, the village girl of *Baiju Bawra*.

Wearing a white sari and a bunch of flowers, Kamal Amrohi's wife arrived at Metro cinema. The sari had been especially prepared for the awards day since my heroine believed that if the occasion was important, a brand-new dress was important. Right through her life, for premieres, awards, etc., she attired herself in virgin unworn garments.

Mr George Allen, the US Ambassador, was chief guest (obviously Indo-US relations were good and not yet disrupted by the Kissinger-Nixon types) and the stately, statuesque award was given to 'Meena for her performance in *Baiju Bawra*' by Mr K.W. Shrouti (who he was nobody seems to know). Other recipients of awards included Dilip Kumar, Naushad and Bimal Roy.

'The day I was honoured with the Filmfare Award,' disclosed my heroine, 'was the most wonderful day in my screen life. On that day I felt rewarded for all the effort I have put into my work since I started acting.' The diplomat in her acknowledged, 'I give my grateful thanks to all those kind people who selected me for this distinction.'

Film-wise, the year 1954 was unrewarding and out of the three films she made, *Badbaan*, *Ilzam* and *Chandni Chowk*, only one was of any virtue, and that was *Chandni Chowk* made by B.R. Chopra—a new name then.

Mr Chopra's maiden effort was faintly encouraging and he tried in his first film to capture the atmosphere of Delhi during the early years of the century. The music was good, the direction showed promise and my heroine was magnificent. 'In a difficult role,' wrote *Filmfare*, 'she turns in a superb portrayal which is alive with feeling and emotions and is an outstanding example of her histrionic talent ... her classic beauty is brilliantly exploited by the photographer of *Chandni Chowk* and he can rightfully claim the honour of presenting the actress of the Indian Screen at her loveliest.' High praise indeed!

Nothing, they say, succeeds like success, and by the middle of 1954 my heroine received another piece of information which left her breathless. She had won the Filmfare 'Best Actress' award for the second year in succession. This time it was for *Parineeta* and she divulged, 'My first award for *Baiju Bawra* was a fluke and I never for a moment believed that the following year too I would receive another award.' Two flukes in a row? No, just ability finding recognition.

In the life of most artistes comes a moment of momentum. A prolific period in which the artiste works and works and works. Command over his craft is such that he becomes its slave—for this craft first demands employment and then satisfaction.

Consequently, in 1955 and many subsequent years my heroine was inundated with assignments.

Now there are two kinds of artistes. Those who revel under the pressure of work and those who revel a little less. Paul Scofield is of the opinion that one film a year is more than sufficient, while Omar Sharif is of the opinion that the more the merrier; my heroine was of the Sharif mould. 'My time is not my own,' she said, 'and the only dates I remember are the dates on which I have to report for work.' Admittedly, there is a note of wistfulness, almost regret, in that statement but I think it is accidental. Meena Kumari loved every minute she was in front of the camera and in 1955 she had seven engagements on hand: *Amar Bani, Bandish, Shatranj, Rukshana, Azad, Adl-e-Jehangir, Mem Sahab*.

Besides my heroine, another personality gaining popularity those days was a gentleman speaking Hindi with traces of Punjabi, called Balraj (the name was later changed to Sunil Dutt). His popularity rested primarily on his ability as a compere/announcer, and he was responsible on 13 March for introducing Meena Kumari to the thousands gathered at Brabourne Stadium for the second Filmfare Awards.

As usual she was dressed in her favourite white sari which had an elegant embroidered border. Morarjee Desai was the chief guest and she accepted her second successive award with typical humility, 'So far as joy is concerned I am undoubtedly overjoyed, but the astonishment at last year's success has multiplied thousandfold. Even now I cannot understand, cannot analyse why I have been honoured again. Now I ask myself with more seriousness than before: What is there in my acting which has made millions of picture-goers bestow on me the certificate of prime popularity?'

My heroine also indicated that although she was grateful and flattered by prime popularity, 'If someone were to ask me, after being honoured for *Baiju Bawra*, whether I deliberately endeavoured to achieve similar results with *Parineeta*, I can honestly say in *Parineeta*, I merely acted.'

Meanwhile, the hit of the year in 1955 was *Azad* and naturally my heroine had a part in it. *Azad*, a tarted-up version of the Robin Hood fable, had Dilip Kumar as the conscientious robber and Meena Kumari as his heart's desire.

One cannot say much about this film except that it was the first my heroine made in that other centre of film production in India—Madras; otherwise, Mr S.M.S. Naidu's effort deserved no aesthetic medals.

Additionally, *Azad* provided her with a small holiday. Most of the shooting for this film took place in Coimbatore and on the day before its conclusion Mr Amrohi flew there (normally he stayed away when Meena went to work either in town or out of town. Usually Baqar or one of the sisters would accompany). In south India, husband and wife played the tourist and visited Rameshwaram, Cape Comorin and other places of historical and religious interest.

The breathtaking scenery and the easy pace of life gave welcome relief to a woman who had been working from sunrise to sunset. For Kamal too these surroundings were inspiration. Mentally he began outlining the plot of his next film and decided that he would call it *Pakeezah*. Two weeks later, Mr and Mrs Amrohi returned to Bombay refreshed and regaled.

At home, life was deliberately quiet. By disposition my heroine was not gregarious. She shunned the vulgar ostentation, the gay parties, the synthetic bonhomie of the film world. Most people considered her a snob; only intimates knew she was genuinely bored by such occasions. Sometimes it was impossible and embarrassing to say no, because the invitations were so insistent and numerous, and occasionally with her husband she would step in and out of some gathering. One such was the wedding of Mr J.C. Jain's daughter in May 1955.

She showed a partiality for premieres though—not because she liked the ceremony and the cordoned crowd, but because she liked going to the movies. And here even when the lights were off there was no shortage of publicity. I am going to give you a piece from a film mag in 1955 only to demonstrate the astounding ability of cinema scribes to make news out of non-news, and also to demonstrate the kind of fodder these journals were dishing out for their readers. Note: 'At a recent premiere a reporter happened to be seated between the petite Nimmi and the lovely Meena Kumari. Said Meena to Nimmi, "I hear you are moving to Bandra. How nice, we'll be neighbours." Whereupon Nimmi pouted, "I'm not sure yet. You see two bedrooms are not enough for me." Just then Dilip Kumar entered the auditorium. It was pitch dark but Dilip seemed to have no difficulty in recognising people. To Nimmi he made a sweeping bow, whereupon the unkissed sweetheart burst out into a giggle. Then he moved to Meena Kumari and raising his hand to his forehead said, "Salama Alekum!"' Is it any wonder that later on in her life she bought a projector to enable her to see movies at home?

A convivial evening for her was a book. Given a few minutes' break in the studio she would open some 'kalam' of an Urdu poet and when called she would turn her book face open downwards on her chair. Work over, she would return to her reading.

How was the marriage going in 1956? I am afraid, not very smoothly, and the first signs of disenchantment were hovering around the previous bliss. My heroine began feeling that her husband's ardours had died a trifle. She felt she was not getting from him the sort of attention she was getting when they were lovers living in separate quarters. Did she miss the telephone calls?

Mr Amrohi says that Meena was imagining things. 'It is impossible after you've lived together for three years to pretend it's still the honeymoon. My love for Meena had not diminished in intensity although I do admit I did not wake up every morning and tell my wife, "I love you." I thought that our relationship was so strong that it required no daily declarations. Obviously I was wrong.'

Trouble was brewing in another area of married life too—work. Before Meena and Kamal signed the vows, Kamal had indicated that once Meena entered his home she would be entering not as Meena but as Mahajabeen, i.e., not as a film star but as a housewife. My heroine, according to Mr Amrohi, agreed to this sacrifice, but requested time. She said that her family then was badly off and once their position was secure she would willingly and gracefully retire, don the apron, buy the vegetables and take up all the duties of an average housewife.

Every man, woman and child in this country should be grateful that my heroine never kept this promise. She had a frank talk with her husband and he told me he was mighty impressed by the manner in which she informed him of her future intentions.

'I accept,' she told Amrohi, 'that before I married you I promised I would retire; but now my work means so much to me that if you insist on me keeping my promise, I shall have to ask you for a divorce.'

Mr Amrohi heard this open statement of intent and realized he was beaten. 'All right,' he said, 'you can continue acting but there will be three conditions: 1) you will return home by 6.30 every evening, 2) you will allow no one in the make-up room except your make-up man, 3) you will sit only in your own car which will take you to work and fetch you back.'

That night my heroine signed on all these terms. The next morning, one by one, she commenced breaking them.

I asked Amrohi whether he was being entirely fair in insisting on these terms. After all she was the most wanted actress of her time and it would have been impossible for her to adhere to such Victorian strictness. 'I didn't mean it like that. These were just ground rules. I mean if she returned home at 7 instead of 6.30 it was acceptable to me. I just wanted her to appreciate that besides having responsibilities to her career she had responsibilities to her home and husband,' he explained. For the moment in 1956 a mutual form of hypocrisy prevailed—both the parties had made their respective positions clear and both the parties knew that their agreement was as durable as the ones they sign at summit conferences.

Professionally, 1956 was a lean year for my heroine. There was quantity but not quality, and the many releases in those twelve months were uniformly tenth-rate. However, no dispute existed about the quality of Meena Kumari, and review after review kept saying that she was 'histrionically incomparable'.

Sharada brought her right back. In every way the film was a hit and this was also the first time that Raj Kapoor and my heroine met on the sets. Both were actors with considerable following and the film couldn't help but be a money-spinner.

I must be honest and disclose that I have not seen *Sharada*, but those who have can hardly sit down. The chief virtue of this film was my heroine who in effect played a sort of double role. In the first half of the film she was Mr Kapoor's heroine, in the second half she was Mr Kapoor's mother.

The story as I have heard it related is so full of tortuous twists and turns that it is barely credible. However, in 1957 no one took issue with this primarily because everyone was too busy singing praises of Meena Kumari, and the manner in which she carried off the role of lover and mother, all in one film.

A friend of mine rang me up recently. He had been told I was writing a book on Meena Kumari. 'Don't forget to mention *Sharada*,' he said, 'it was her greatest film.'

Possibly he was exaggerating, but *Sharada* did win further wide acclaim for my heroine. By now of course nobody doubted the ability of Meena Kumari and everybody began expecting of her an expertise, a class, which stood above the others. If my heroine was good, it was not surprising for the public. She now had a standard to live up to and she never faltered.

While my heroine as an actress was securely on top, her marriage was steadily going downhill. Rancour, suspicion and a certain degree of childishness were the contributing factors. Amrohi demanded allegiance to his three conditions which Meena broke with joyful abandon.

During the shooting of *Sharada* at R.K. Studio, Raj Kapoor

invited Meena for a party. A Russian film delegation was in town and Mr Kapoor was hosting a reception for Mr Khrushchev's comrades. Meena accepted the invitation and telephoned her husband saying she would be late. The reason she gave was not the party but work. Coincidentally, that very morning Kamal met a few guests who were also invited to the Russian reception. Thus the husband knew that his wife was not working overtime but engaged in festivities.

Neither did Meena say anything when she returned home that night. Subsequently, when Amrohi confronted her with the harmless deceit, she simply said it was of no consequence and she had suppressed it because she did not wish to disturb him.

Something similar occurred with Pradeep Kumar. He had purchased a new Chrysler and invited my heroine for a spin. She being a great motor fan agreed and enjoyed the ride in the imported jalopy. However, when she came close to Bandra she removed herself from the foreign car, summoned a taxi, and went home in this public vehicle. Of course, as luck would have it, she was caught in the process of changing cars by Baqar.

In the make-up room, which Amrohi had conditioned as out of bounds for all except the make-up man, my heroine welcomed and entertained visitors openly. Inevitably, news of this reached Amrohi. He says his wife never once said to him, 'So-and-so was in my make-up room today.'

And this was his grouse. He told me that he was prepared to overlook Meena bending his conditions but he would have loved if she herself confessed when such bendings took place. 'It really pained me to learn of these incidents from outside sources.'

On the face of it the causes of the conflict seem so frivolous that one cannot accept them as the real causes. Something deeper, more sinister, was at work and Mr Amrohi discovered this when making his wife's bed.

That very day she had left town on a shooting assignment and forgotten to take her diary which Amrohi discovered under her pillow.

Now, ever since she could write, Meena was in the habit of keeping a record. This was not strictly a diary, more a scrap book. Famous sayings, favourite poetry, Marilyn Monroe, personal observations were all combined in this collage. (It was much later that she did away with the frills and began keeping a conventional diary.)

Anyway, Mr Amrohi discovered a black book and his first reaction was to put it away unopened. This he did on the first day but on the second he couldn't keep his hands off it. Despite my prodding, Amrohi refused to divulge the contents of this diary. He did tell me however that when he read his wife's work his 'hair stood up'. One sentence in this diary he did share with me. It appears somewhere on the pages my heroine had written, 'I have never loved Kamal Amrohi.'

On Meena's return, Kamal Amrohi told her that she had forgotten a part of her baggage, and handed over the diary.

That night, husband and wife had a heart-to-heart talk. 'Was anything wrong?' Kamal asked. Meena said no except that she was a little tired.

Months began rolling by, the misunderstandings continued to mount, and domestic life reached a stalemate. My heroine progressed smoothly with her career and in 1959 starred in another big success, *Chirag Kahan Roshni Kahan*, with Rajendra Kumar.

Mr Rajendra Kumar was a recent find. He had only just made his debut on the screen; under Meena Kumari's benign tutelage he became a star in his own right. A year earlier she had performed a similar miracle for Sunil Dutt in a film called *Ek Hi Rasta*.

Had she become so powerful now that she could make or break stars? The answer is yes. Those who took protection under her shadow were the automatic recipients of reflected glory. Way back in her time, my heroine had been shown consideration, and similarly, she adopted an attitude of guardian, artistic mentor and friend towards the new boys. Initially, the Rajendra Kumars and Sunil Dutts were in cold sweat at the prospect of working with such a dazzling star, and if she wanted—and they knew this—she could have bullied them, humiliated them and screwed up their careers. But that would have been out of character. Instead, she went out of her way to guide those struggling to make the mark.

Three films of Meena Kumari were released in the year 1960. Two out of these were mammoth hits while the third was not so mammoth. *Dil Apna Aur Preet Parayi*[3] and *Kohinoor*, the two successes, were entirely different in nature. *Kohinoor* was one of the few comedies my heroine made and its sale was assured by its stars: Dilip Kumar and Meena Kumari. *Dil Apna* was a different proposition. The story of a dedicated nurse unable to marry the doctor she loved, and torn between the noble ideals of her craft and her innate desires, was produced for the screen by the husband and directed by Kishore Sahu. Meena played the nurse sacrificing everything for the glory of Florence Nightingale. Among my heroine's admirers there is lively controversy whether this portrayal was the finest of her acting life.

---

3 It appears Amrohi thought this film to be so bad that he didn't want it released.

Meanwhile, domestic life found another source of disharmony: 'Basi Rotis' (chapattis left overnight). It appears that she had an old fondness for this kind of wheat which some people consider a delicacy while others consider unhealthy. And she was constantly having difficulty obtaining these in Mr Amrohi's house. 'I told her that Rembrandt was her house and if she wanted basi rotis, all she had to do was place an order in the kitchen. For myself, I think it is bad to eat such food but if Meena really wanted this she just had to lift her finger,' Mr Amrohi explained to me.

The basi roti crisis came to a head at one luncheon meeting. Kamal and Meena were about to begin their midday meal when my heroine told her husband, 'How unfortunate I am. All I want is basi roti and I can't even get that.' To drive home this point she shouted across to the kitchen.

'Is there any basi roti?'

'No, memsahab,' replied the cook.

'See,' my heroine said to Mr Amrohi.

These matrimonial difficulties seem so trivial that they instantly confirm my original thinking. Meena Kumari and Kamal Amrohi were so far apart now that even the most proficient marriage counsellor would have declined the job of bringing them together.

One man who had been watching Meena Kumari films with more than professional interest was Guru Dutt. Like my heroine he too was someone who had seen the lean and the fat. In his personal life he was of extravagant tastes. Profligate, weary and genius, he had long been toying with a film idea. Previously he had won a few rounds with the audience, but the demands of the commercial cinema were weighing him down. Consequently, he decided to try *Sahib Bibi Aur Ghulam* and make peace with his true creative urges.

Together with friend Abrar Alvi he polished and repolished the script, gathered a cast, recorded the songs, printed the posters.

There was, however, one major gap. An important, indeed pivot, role had not been assigned. Chhoti Bahu, the heroine of the film, was nowhere to be found. In his own mind, Guru Dutt was certain that if there was one woman who could bring credit to this part it was my heroine. And do you know she nearly missed it?

Guru Dutt sent word that he would be interested in hiring my heroine. Was she available? The answer from Rembrandt was no, she had her hands full with pending commitments.

Some Indian girl living and acting in London was sent an air ticket and she arrived for the initial takes. But she was entirely unsuitable and further completely unsympathetic to the part. In desperation, Guru Dutt sent for the clapper boy and commenced rolling his camera, and by the beginning of 1962 the whole film was in the can except Chhoti Bahu.

Negotiations with Meena Kumari were resumed and this time they were more successful. Forty-five clear and consecutive days were offered and the fee raised by 25 per cent. Guru Dutt agreed to all provisions and my heroine began shooting at Natraj Studios[4] in Andheri.

A Walter Mathau quote is relevant here: 'Every actor all his life looks for a part that will combine his talents with his personality.' Meena found such a part, and for myself I am convinced that it was the part of her life. Of the mountainous films Meena made, her performance in *Sahib Bibi* stands on the pinnacle. If I wish to remember my heroine as a film star I wish to remember her as Guru Dutt's Chhoti Bahu.

---

4 Then called Kamal Studios. Mr Amrohi and Guru Dutt were half owners, but they never got on well.

Everything was right for this film. The earnestness, the challenge, the excitement of honest creativity, the professionalism, all engendered an atmosphere wonderfully conducive to serious work.

Why she accepted Guru Dutt's offer Allah only knows. In every way the role he had offered her was so remote from her experience, so full of subtle nuances, so damaging to her public image, so impossible, that I am positive no other Bombay actress would have touched it. She was a little nervous herself as she drove to work the first day. 'I feel uneasy about things. But it is an uneasiness I like. Once again after a long time, I am feeling as if I am going to face the camera for the first time. *Sahib Bibi Aur Ghulam* pages have engulfed me entirely.' Bengali decadence was the theme of this film—moral, physical and spiritual. And both Meena Kumari and Guru Dutt showed an uncommon command over the grammar of this decadence. Sometimes riveting, sometimes revolting, the flesh triumphed over the spirit in *Sahib Bibi* to demonstrate that unadulterated virtue is a lie. Yet, and kudos for this to Guru Dutt and Abrar Alvi, all the characters—from the degenerate nawab to the simpleton Bhootnath—were drawn with a strong sense of reality and a tender appreciation of human folly.

My tragedienne was now thirty-two and at the height of her powers. In every frame of *Sahib Bibi* she fills the screen with her presence (remember the competition: Waheeda Rehman, Guru Dutt, Rehman) and quietly walks away with the histrionics.

In the first half she is the conventional housewife determined to be a devoted Hindu spouse. Now this is not a part which allows much acting scope, but Chhoti Bahu walks around with such unruffled dignity that you feel the woman must have been a Bengali housewife all her life.

Restraint as a performing quality is virtually unknown to Indian actors, and Meena Kumari was among the solitary who understood and practised it. In one unforgettable frame she tells Guru Dutt with whispered pathos that the Hindu woman has but one ambition in life, and that is to serve her husband till her last breath; a pernicious ambition but from Chhoti Bahu it comes out with a force and conviction which is both gripping and engaging.

And it wasn't easy. My heroine wrote in her private diary: 'This woman is troubling me a great deal. All day long—and a good part of the night—it is nothing else but Chhoti Bahu's helplessness. Chhoti Bahu's sorrows, Chhoti Bahu's smiles, Chhoti Bahu's hopes, Chhoti Bahu's tribulations, Chhoti Bahu's endurance, Chhoti Bahu's … Chhoti Bahu's … Chhoti Bahu … Oh! I am sick of it.'

Beautiful. How beautiful she appeared. For once the camera captured my heroine, and did justice to a face that was now at its zenith. Gone were the traces of frivolity, gone was the look of undernourishment, gone was the look of the 'girl next door'. She was now a woman of sharp, mature, mysterious persona; a woman whose one smile concealed a thousand enigmas.

I think back to a sequence lasting four minutes in *Sahib Bibi* where Meena has acquired a love potion to lure her husband's affections, and is seen in the many stages of adornment. The sequence begins with Meena completely undecked and as each shot progresses, a garment and a piece of jewellery is added to her person. This culminates in a final shot and glory, my heroine is on the screen fully dressed. You probably think this is a biographer gone mad but I have not seen in Indian cinema a face more beautiful than I saw in those few seconds.

But this was just a foretaste of things to come. It was in

the second part of Guru Dutt's film that my heroine gave the performance of her life.

Rehman, her husband, an honest to goodness lecher goes out in search of dancing girls each night and my heroine suggests he stay at home. 'Will you drink with me,' he asks tauntingly, 'will you laugh, sing and dance for me.' She recoils at the thought and that very night orders her first drink ... and her next ... and her next.

If there is a hackneyed role in our cinema it is the role of the alcoholic. There are some standard movements and motions to go through and most of our actors have learned these off like parrots. Motilal was the only one who knew what it was to be inebriated and he never shouted or blared or fell into a gutter. (Drunks usually become more conscious of their movement and tend to be quiet rather than loud.)

For a person who in her private life knew nothing about the bottle (she had not started drinking yet) she understood 'nasha' remarkably well. She had help though. 'I discussed Chhoti Bahu with Kamal Sahab till late at night. Before this, Kamal Sahab had appreciated *Parineeta*, *Badbaan*, *Sharada*, but he had never advised me how to interpret a role. Today for the first time he explained to me what all types of behaviour a drunken but repressed and helpless woman can assume,' she scribbled in her diary.

In one scene, glass in hand, she explains to Guru Dutt why she has taken to whisky. The explanation is not unique but the expression on her face is. 'Do you think I like this?' she says pointing to the glass and then in reply curls up her face and vomits pegs of revulsion.

The pièce de résistance of my heroine in *Sahib Bibi*, however, is a song. And as a true connoisseur I think that sequence of

film should be preserved in the archives. Currently we hear
and see a lot about Mr B.R. Ishara and sexy films (the two by
now being synonymous), and some of the hilarious lengths our
producers go to undress their leading lads and ladies is nothing
short of ingenious. (Usually it rains and the couple is caught
unawares. Nearby is a hotel. They hang their clothes in front
of the fire, wrap themselves up in long towels and presto, the
next thing you know Hema Malini is pregnant.) Mr Ishara and
Co. should go and see my heroine dish out bosomfuls of sex
without the aid of a single towel in Guru Dutt's 1962 film.

Great friends, Abrar Alvi and Guru Dutt nearly came apart
over picturizing this immortal 1,000 feet. Most of the film
Mr Dutt had left to Alvi. However, the scenes in which my
heroine, slightly tipsy, sings to Rehman he wanted for himself.
Women and wine were two areas where his expertise was
universally unchallenged and he felt confident that he was
more qualified than his friend to supervise this sequence. In a
fit of pique, Alvi left the studio saying that if his services were
required further he would be found at home.

The situation was really quite simple. My heroine tries to
hold her husband from his nightly debauchery and sings a
song (a song, incidentally, which haunted Guru Dutt all his
subsequent life). However, it was not the melody but the
delicate, tasteful, lascivious Meena Kumari wooing which
made this tune into a minor sexual feast. Biting her man's ear,
ruffling his hair, caressing his neck, running her hands over
his kurta, she created an environment of pulsating, titillating
and mouth-watering sexuality.

Mind you the year was 1962 and the audiences unused to
display of erotica. Fresh bouquets therefore for both Guru Dutt
and my heroine for being years ahead of time, and for setting
up a prototype for our present-day screen perverts.

There was delicious dichotomy. Although the audiences accepted sexuality on the bed they did not accept it on the horse carriage, and a complete segment with a Hemant Kumar song in the background had to be cut one day after the release of the film. Before she is murdered, my heroine goes out on a late-night drive and in the carriage rests her head on Guru Dutt's sympathetic lap. This was the offending portion and it was quickly scissored. Two days of hasty shooting enabled Guru Dutt to insert something more innocuous.

The people who had made Sahib Bibi were prepared for a financial disaster. Both the treatment and the subject were not commercial, and no one could predict which way this film would go. Consequently, Guru Dutt and his backers were pleasantly surprised at the queues they saw outside Minerva cinema in Bombay.

Money started rolling in, and not only was the investment salvaged but the producers were able to make a bit on the side too. Sahib Bibi was no Baiju Bawra but it proved that ambition, courage and imagination do not necessarily spell disaster for the adventurous film-maker. In a sense today's much talked about 'New Wave' actually started in 1962.

If the first two years of Meena Kumari's married life were absolute bliss, the last two years of her married life were absolute hell. And if previously the causes had been trivial, they were not so now, and some very fundamental husband and wife incompatibilities, long suppressed, surfaced.

For example at Eros cinema. Mr and Mrs Amrohi had been invited for a big premiere by Sohrab Modi. Bombay's Rotary Club–type dignitaries were present when Mr Modi introduced my heroine to the governor of Maharashtra. 'This is the renowned actress Meena Kumari,' he said, 'and this is her husband Kamal Amrohi.' Whereupon, before namastes could be exchanged, Amrohi interjected, 'No. I am Kamal Amrohi and this is my wife, the renowned film actress Meena Kumari.' Saying this he left the auditorium. My heroine saw the premiere alone.

Sahib Bibi was selected as the Indian entry to the Berlin Film Festival and Meena, who as yet had not stepped outside the shores of her country, was selected as a delegate. The then minister of information arranged for two tickets—one for my heroine and one for her husband. But he refused to go. 'Why should I,' he said, 'I have made no contribution to the selected film. I am neither its director nor its writer. I don't want to tag along merely as Meena Kumari's husband.' Graciously, he did not stop his wife and offered to send Baqar as chaperon.

The trip never materialized but it did indicate an attitude. Meena felt that her husband was sulking. She had no sympathies with Amrohi's embittered ego.

For it was nothing but an ego clash. Kamal Amrohi was a man of no mean self-importance. One of the finest writers of Urdu, he had begun to feel that his only function in life was to organize film dates for his wife—sort of manager. To most people he had ceased to be Kamal Amrohi the famed inventor of *Mahal*; instead, he had become the husband of the famed Meena Kumari—a character out of Von Sternberg's *Blue Angel*. To me he was charmingly honest. 'This is true, that looking after Meena became for me a full-time job, and where as an artiste she steadily climbed upwards, I steadily climbed downwards.'

Amrohi is somewhat unfair. My heroine did not set out deliberately to destroy his fame or career. And it was no fault of hers if she climbed steadily upwards. Although I must confess I can understand his sense of bitterness and his behaviour at the Eros premiere. Of all the Amrohi matrimonial conditions the one I find most touching and most revealing concerns motor cars. Meena, living up to her status, had acquired a new Mercedes but Mr Amrohi refused to step inside. 'When you go to your studio, you can go in your Mercedes, but when you go with me you will have to sit inside my old Buick.'

Poor Kamal, he could never have imagined that the little girl he had met at Sassoon Hospital would one day become such a glittering star that she would wipe the shine clean off his star.

It is difficult to fix the exact date when my heroine took to drink. Always a creature of the night, she was a veritable owl—the difference being that she did not sleep in the day either—who since the days of her telephone romance had found difficulty in closing her eyes. Dr Saeed Timurza, her physician, then prescribed a peg of brandy as a sleeping pill, and this was officially how she came into contact with the habit that was to kill her.

If she took to drink initially it was because she was exhausted. (According to Kamal Amrohi, the one peg of brandy increased to many more. One day he apprehended Meena's maidservant pouring out the doctor's medicine and he noticed the glass was nearly half full. On reprimanding the maidservant he discovered that this measure had become my heroine's standard, and further, the bottles of Dettol in the Amrohi bathroom did not contain antiseptic but brandy. From that day onwards Kamal says he checked the Dettol bottles and ensured that Meena did not have any drink handy.)

However devoted one may be to one's vocation, there is a physical limit, and Meena was working so remorselessly that I am surprised she did not have a physical breakdown. In the years 1962–63 she had sixteen contracts on hand and she confessed, 'Every morning as I leave the house for the studios a weariness fills me. I say to myself, "Let this be the last ride. Let me come back in the evening, pack up my things and go for a long holiday."'

I wish she had. Instead, she continued working like a Trojan while things at Rembrandt deteriorated still further.

Squabbles, arguments, bad feeling, drink—and now physical violence.

Unexpectedly, it all began on the auspicious day of Eid. On that night Meena's feelings for her husband were such that she grabbed his 'chikan kurta' by the neck and ripped it. Amrohi says that he too lost his temper and for the first time, as he puts it, 'lifted his hand'. (Whether he lifted his hand for the first time or not I shall discuss later.)

Allow me to digress a little.

The life of a popular film star is such that it demands at all times a composed public face. Since a film star is the property of the public, he must, whatever his private circumstances, maintain his social obligations. To her fans, therefore, it was of no consequence whether Meena Kumari was having boxing bouts with her husband or whether she was drinking brandy out of Dettol bottles or whether she desperately wanted a respite from the camera. No, for them she was the ace actress of India and her behind-the-screen tribulations had no admirers.

Commensurately, she went around performing opening ceremonies of exhibitions, attending things like the Amber Glow Ball (admittedly this was for a worthy cause: the National Defence Fund), visiting premieres in the smiling company of the man (Kamal Amrohi) she was hardly on speaking terms with, blessing newly-wed second cousins of cinema distributors, picking out fifty contest winners for *Filmfare*. The show, as they say, must go on. Of course film stars always complain, 'Look these are the kind of sacrifices we have to make. Life for us is not one big dream come true. Actually we would love to be anonymous.' They lie. If there is one thing our matinee idols revel in, it is publicity. (Shashi Kapoor once told me that it was a lovely feeling being mobbed on the road.) And if you are going to be a popular film star, you have no right to expect a private life—just as Mrs Gandhi has no right to expect a private life. It is impossible to appear on the cover of *Star and Style* and at the same time hope to enter a restaurant unnoticed. And show me a film star who would give up the cover of *Star and Style* for the privilege of entering a restaurant quietly.

Life is not completely unfair. If things are going badly in one sphere, they are invariably going well in the other. On 5 April 1963 the shortlist was in for the Filmfare Awards and Meena Kumari created a record—a record which I suspect will remain for a long time to come. The three female performances of 1962 contending for the 'Best Actress' were: Meena Kumari in *Sahib Bibi Aur Ghulam*, Meena Kumari in *Aarti*, Meena Kumari in *Main Chup Rahungi*. Victory for my heroine was ensured and the only doubt remained which performance. It was *Sahib Bibi Aur Ghulam*.

In Bombay on 13 June it was raining and the Indian Navy band especially hired for the occasion had to move inside Regal cinema. The occasion was the tenth Filmfare Awards, and besides, Governor Vijaya Lakshmi Pandit was present as the chief guest.

My heroine, the magazines noticed, 'looked like a picture of grace'. The white sari was conspicuous, so was the white purse, so were the glistening pearls hanging from her exquisite ears. She accepted her third award from Mrs Pandit and said, 'No words can describe how happy I am today.'

Later, she delighted a packed audience with a recitation of Faiz Ahmed Faiz's poems. The voice that had enchanted millions of cinema-goers in India held the VIPs spellbound. Immediately afterwards, they lined up to felicitate her. The next morning Lux toilet soap, old fans, took out large advertisements in leading papers indicating their approval of my heroine.

One of the films Meena was working in at this time was Bimal Roy's *Benazir*. The assistant director and lyric writer was a gentleman called Gulzar, an Urdu poet and writer seduced like many others into the film world. My heroine immediately struck a chord with Mr Gulzar. A poet and writer herself, she found the company of another poet and writer both stimulating and relaxing. Between takes they would talk about books, the writing of diaries and Mir.[5] The company of Gulzar also provided a welcome antidote to life at home. It was essentially a relationship of the spirit rather than of the flesh. When Gulzar was not present or Meena was working elsewhere, the telephone served as the connecting link.

Amrohi says that it was at *Benazir* that his marriage was finally ruined. The Bimal Roy group (consisting of Salil Chowdhury, Achla Sachdev, etc.) and the Mehmood group were instrumental in filling the ears of my heroine, and were the chief perpetrators of this felony.

Much love was never lost between Bimal Roy and Amrohi. Mr Roy had earlier approached Kamal for signing Meena in a

---

5 Nineteenth-century Urdu poet.

film called *Devdas* (Suchitra Sen got the role) and Mr Amrohi
rejected the offer. Subsequently, when Bimal Roy met my
heroine he asked her why she had refused such a peach of a
part. 'I know nothing about it. I would have loved to play it,'
she replied.

Anyway, the story goes that the Bimal Roy and the
Mehmood groups provided fuel for fire: 'He is using you.
Don't you see you are nothing but a moneymaking machine
for him. You are India's most wanted actress and what have
you to show for it. All your money is going to Kamal Amrohi.
Leave him, you'll be better off.' This was the sound advice my
heroine received and she considered it carefully.

By the end of 1963, Meena Kumari had decided to leave
Kamal Amrohi—and he knew it.

One morning, just before my heroine was off to work, Mr
Amrohi went into the bedroom. He took hold of his wife's
face and said, 'Manju don't leave me.'

It was too late for reconciliation. Meena, in the second
month of 1964, began moving her luggage surreptitiously to
the house of Achla Sachdev, and really there was only one
thing missing—the showdown.

The second landmark in my heroine's life is 5 March
1964.

The mahurat for *Pinjre Ke Panchhi* was scheduled at 11 a.m.
on this date. Mr Baqar Ali and his wife arrived early to ensure
that arrangements were satisfactory. Satisfied, they called
Bertha, the hair dresser, and told her that no one was to be
allowed inside Meena Kumari's make-up room today. These
were strict instructions, Baqar informed Bertha, and had to be
scrupulously obeyed.

It was 11.30 a.m. and Meena had not arrived. She was

holding up the ceremony. A little nervousness became apparent and those connected with the film suggested that enquiries be made regarding the whereabouts of my heroine.

In bad temper she arrived almost immediately and went straight in the direction of her make-up room. En route she was accosted by Bertha who, instead of keeping the Baqar instructions to herself, divulged them to Meena. Already in bad temper, she was now furious and summoned Gulzar. Baqar was also in the vicinity and when she saw him she wished a most unfriendly 'adab'.

Three people then, Meena, Baqar and Gulzar began walking towards the make-up room which was situated above a flight of stairs. The fateful journey began.

Before I come to the actual incident that sparked off the dissociation, let me state that there are at least ten different versions of 'exactly what happened'. The two most important of these—the Baqar and Meena versions—really concern us and I shall give you both.

The positioning, going up the stairs, played a vital part. Meena led, followed by Baqar followed by Gulzar. To begin with, the journey was peaceful but just before the stairs concluded my heroine looked back and indicated to Gulzar that his presence was required in the private chamber. Gulzar, sensing trouble and unsure, made no positive move, and my heroine again looked back and this time rather strongly said, 'What are you waiting for?' Emboldened, Gulzar moved and attempted to overtake Baqar. Baqar intervened and stopped his progress. Gulzar was thus stuck most uncomfortably in the middle.

A bit of pushing and jostling took place and then Meena burst out in a tremendous rage. Screaming at the top of her voice she faced Baqar, 'Who do you think I am? Do you think I am a whore? What goes on in my make-up room that you have placed such restrictions?' Saying which she clutched Mr Gulzar to her bosom.

At this point, my heroine claims Baqar slapped her. Mr Baqar claims he did no such thing and told me he was prepared to take an oath to this effect. Nargis who was shooting in the adjacent set says that she heard a great deal of noise and also heard Baqar shouting, who for his part says that he tried his utmost to pacify Meena and also solicited aid from Mr Balraj Sahni, an observer of this scene. Either way, the onlookers and guests at the mahurat saw the usually composed Meena Kumari in tantrums. Crying copiously, she breezed out of the studio, informing Baqar, 'Tell Kamal Sahab I will not be coming home tonight.' She kept her word.

FOUR

Fall

Look what happened to her (Meena) after she left my home.

– Kamal Amrohi

Storming out of the mahurat, my heroine went to see her
friend Rajni Patel.[1] In consultation with Mr Patel it was decided
that Meena use her sister's house as temporary residence, till
such time something more suitable could be found. Mr Patel
also offered the services of his assistant, Mr Kishore Sharma
(later to marry Madhu), in organizing the details.

Sharma rang up Madhu and also spoke to Mehmood,
the husband. Both were enthusiastic to the idea of a guest.
However, Mehmood suggested to Mr Sharma not to deposit
Meena immediately but after midnight. The motive for this
delay was that Mehmood had numerous other guests in the
house and he wanted to dispose of them before welcoming my
heroine. Kishore Sharma too thought that a late-night entry
would be a good idea.

---

1 Now the president of the BPCC.

Before she went to Andheri, however, she went to the law and registered a complaint. At the station she made a four-line statement saying that she had reason to believe that her life was in danger. A good tax-paying citizen, she demanded police protection.

On his side, Baqar went back to Rembrandt and gave his master a blow-by-blow account of the proceedings at *Pinjre Ke Panchhi*. Having heard, Mr Amrohi laughed. 'We'll sort the whole thing out when she comes home this evening,' he said optimistically.

This evening came but not my heroine. Around 8.30, Kamal got the jitters. Possibly he was underestimating the seriousness of the incident? But where could he go searching? Telephone calls were made to the studio and to the houses of mutual friends but they offered no clue. 'She could be just driving around,' reflected Mr Amrohi, and presently Baqar and son and Amrohi began a search of Bombay. It was like looking for Meena in a haystack.

They drove through Gateway of India, they went to Hanging Gardens, they looked at Juhu beach—but my heroine was not in sight.

As a last-ditch attempt they went looking to Mehmood's house, in Andheri, and here the search came to an end—Amrohi sighted two or three policemen. Meena was probably in. When the others in the car offered to join Amrohi in his patching-up expedition, he said categorically, 'No. This is my business. I'll go alone.'

He walked towards the house and asked the policemen patrolling the nature of their duty. Just as he was being told, Mehmood came out and was exceedingly civil. 'Is Manju here?'

Amrohi enquired. Mr Mehmood truthfully said yes, but she
was in a room upstairs, resting. 'I would like to speak to her,'
demanded the husband. Mehmood requested my heroine's
husband to please come back some other time. Madhu, who
had also come out by now, added her voice to this request.
'Please tell her I wish to speak to her,' Kamal persisted. Madhu
went up bearing the message.

Ten minutes later she returned with an answer. My heroine
informed her husband that she did not desire audience with
him—at least not on that night. Mr Amrohi says he went
up to the stairs to the room himself. He tried to open. It
was closed. He knocked. And knocked again, but the door
remained firmly shut.

Standing outside the closed door, Chandan called out to his
wife, 'Manju, there is no fight between you and me. You have
had a fight with Baqar, and I promise you that after today Baqar
will not step inside my home. Before this whole thing gets out
of hand, before people come to know, let us return home. Look,
I have come to apologize and take you back.' Having said his
piece, Kamal waited for either a reply or the loosening of the
bolt. Neither happened, only Mr Mehmood came up and said
that this matrimonial disturbance was certain to be noticed by
his neighbours. It would be best for Mr Amrohi to leave Meena
alone for the moment. 'Today only your neighbours notice,'
thundered Kamal, 'tomorrow the whole world will notice.'

Kamal made one more attempt to open communications.
My heroine's locked room had an extension telephone and Mr
Amrohi rang the number. It kept ringing without being picked
up. Madhu was again sent up, this time to ascertain whether
Manju would consent to talk to her Chandan on the telephone.
She came back with a negative reply. Kamal recovered for a

minute and then informed Madhu, 'I will never come to collect Manju again.' He too kept his word.

My heroine's stubbornness bordering on discourtesy had justification. Since she had irrevocably decided to leave her husband's house, Meena thought it futile to open dialogue with him. Also, not being a particularly strong-willed person she thought she might succumb to Kamal's sweet tongue. For her it was best to keep the door shut.

Madhu and Mehmood had a house in Andheri with the ambitious name of 'Paradise'. It was large, it was patrolled by ferocious dogs and it housed thirty-eight people, all relatives of Mr Mehmood.

On the top floor of this house, a fairly large and comfortable room was allotted to my heroine. It had all the material comforts of a single room with the added luxury of an extension telephone. On the face of it, this makeshift accommodation appeared suitable, and additionally Meena felt secure because she was in touch with close relatives.

Mr Sharma told me that all Meena had on 5 March 1964 was 500 rupees plus the clothes on her person. The Amrohi testimony forwards that Manju not only removed most of her belongings but also withdrew most of her money from the bank before she left. In a most untypical outburst she is supposed to have said before she left Rembrandt, 'I'll make sure that Kamal and his sons starve on the streets of Bombay.'

Much later, on 25 August 1968, Chandan posted to his Manju a letter in which he raised some of these points. '... but only an infinite complaint is left in the corner of my heart: you didn't tell me why you didn't come back to the house after your fight with Baqar Sahab. You yourself had written two days before you left, "Baqar Sahab, you are like my father and elder brother." This little thing keeps pricking my heart. Well anyway ... time will put a dust on this even one day. By the way I have one favour to ask of you. If you have any feeling in your heart left for me, take all these riches and gifts and free me from the allegation that I looted you for my benefit and put you on the footpath with just three clothes.'

Three clothes or four, my heroine was soon in the money again. With Mehmood and his relatives she signed *Chandan Ka Palna*, while working on four other assignments, including *Chitralekha*—a film which Amrohi was bitterly opposed to.

Around now a name called Dharmendra was being bandied about. This man had come from the Punjab to make a name for himself with the sort of determination one reads in storybooks. Not deterred by the fact that thousands with ambitions similar to his arrive in Bombay every month, he stuck to his resolve. With worn soles, an empty stomach and no chance of nepotism (Mr Dharmendra had no uncle in the cinema industry), he made a daily round of the studios hoping for a sale. What kept him going was his grit, a stubborn persistence, a faith that finally he would be spotted.

Incidentally, he knew nothing about acting, neither did he look like Cary Grant. What he did have was a earthy, slightly primitive, woodcutter charm. One look at him and you knew he was a product of 'asli ghee' (pure ghee).

Dharmendra got his breaks—but alas he nearly made a disaster of them. His first film was a total failure and in subsequent efforts he showed no discernible talent. Fortunately, *Shola Aur Shabnam*, although a box-office failure, was pleasantly noticed and got moderate praise from the critics.

And then the best thing that ever happened to Dharmendra

happened—he met my heroine, and his entire life from that day onwards took a different direction.

The film they were signed on together was called *Purnima*, and Dharmendra would go around asking, 'What is Meenaji like?' He was petrified at the prospect of facing her in front of the camera.

Cast opposite an established star, the novice is surrounded with handicaps. Having got his break he must on the one hand prove himself in his own right, and on the other extract a quantum of respect from the established star. (My heroine was too absorbed an artiste for malice, but some of the others are known openly to interfere in the casting.)

At *Purnima*, therefore, Dharmendra was unsteady. He approached someone who had worked with my heroine for solace and advice. 'It's no joke,' said this man, 'playing opposite Meena Kumari without letting her completely overshadow you. She can outclass you without a line of dialogue, with a mere twitch of her lips, or glance. If I were you, I would simply go and touch her feet before facing the camera.' For a man who was already unsteady, this advice wasn't much help.

A serious student of Hindi cinema, Dharmendra had his own personal list of favourites. My heroine occupied top place in this list. As a result, this particular novice approached *Purnima* with the right amount of humility and willingness to learn. 'I had always been an ardent fan of Meenaji. I used to see her pictures and worship her. It was my ambition to become an actor, and it was my dream to act opposite Meenaji.' The note of reverence in this statement is of consequence for it played an important part later on.

Face-to-face they came for the first time at Chandivili

during outdoor shooting. 'Naturally, I was a bit nervous and apprehensive. But when I was introduced to her, she was warm and friendly and welcomed me with kind encouragement. I was thrilled, happy and gratified.'

My heroine on her part liked Dharmendra, I am told, at first sight. There is no confirmation whether he touched her feet, but there is confirmation that she said, 'This boy will rise. He is not the routine entry.'

Coincidentally, at this particular moment of her life, Meena Kumari required a stable and devoted man: big and strong, someone on whom she could literally rest her head, and someone who was not too famous.

One of Mr Dharmendra's associates who watched this relationship flower is on record, 'In the beginning it was primarily work between them. Meenaji would spend all her spare time to enact Dharmendra's scenes for him. With patience and affection she would explain each and every detail of the shot, put him right when he did something unsuitably, make him practise his part until he was perfect and natural. She helped him correct his weak points, while developing his abilities. She inspired confidence in the uncertain youth. She was the stimulus.'

Two aspects deserve attention here.

One, Meena got a certain kick in picking up people struggling in the industry. These strugglers were invariably male and young. 'She always liked having a few puppies around her,' was how someone close to my heroine put it.

Two, 'grooming and correcting weak points' had an ulterior motive. Really it was a ploy. Meena Kumari wished to engage the attention of this young man. She was too dignified and renowned an actress to make an open pass; therefore, by feigning professional interest she was initially able to spend time with Dharmendra without making her real intentions known to him or to others. Nothing wrong, just good gamesmanship.

Existence at Paradise meanwhile was far from heavenly. It appeared she had exchanged one cage for another. The inmates at Mehmood's house made it their business to scrutinize and examine everything and anything that came for my heroine—mail, telephones, visitors. Nobody was allowed to see her and she felt totally isolated in her room.

Salma Sidiqqi, a very dear friend of Meena, attempted to get in touch with her on the telephone at Mehmood's house. Her account of this telephone call and of a subsequent visit to Paradise substantiates the inconveniences my heroine faced at her brother-in-law's residence:

'When I telephoned Mehmood's house I got no satisfactory answer about Meena. Nobody was prepared to tell anything. Instead, questions regarding my profession, my reason for telephoning, my father's name, etc. were asked.'

Later, Salma suggested to Krishan Chander[2] that they go and see Meena unannounced. Krishan Chander was not too keen. 'If she can't come on the telephone,' he said, 'how can you just go to her house.'

Finally, they went to see Meena, and outside the house the interrogation started again. Who are you? What do you want? Why have you come? Additionally, some dogs appeared on the horizon. The visitors were scared. Fortunately, my heroine heard the commotion, came out and rescued her guests.

Informed sources say that Mr Mehmood himself was not responsible for the discourtesies, but those around him were.

---

2 Noted Urdu writer.

My heroine anyway had no intentions of staying for any length with her brother-in-law, and she instructed Kishore Sharma to search for new accommodation. He succeeded and found a place in Juhu.

'Janki Kutir' looks somewhat like Disneyland. A quaint cluster of minute cottages, small meandering mud lanes, close-cropped hedges, expansive green lawns, all invest this area with science-fiction charm. My first reaction when I saw Janki Kutir was: is it real?

In late August 1964, after a total stay of five months in Andheri, Meena Kumari moved to Juhu.

The occupants in the new house were not few. My heroine's stepsister and her children moved in and so did other relatives. They were all supposed to look after Meena. Although this house was large, Amrohi told me that on the only occasion he went there he thought he 'had come to a zoo. There were so many people peering from windows, from behind the curtains, I estimated at least twenty-five people were living with Manju then.'

Two significant and unexpected occupants at Janki Kutir were Madhu and Kishore Sharma. Madhu's marriage with Mehmood was on the rocks and during Meena's stay at Andheri, Madhu frequently met Kishore Sharma. Mr Sharma is a man of many parts. 'I don't drink. I don't eat meat. I am an astrologer, a palmist and a philosopher,' is how he describes himself.

Madhu's regard for Sharma deepened to the extent that she left Mehmood and moved in with Meena. So did Mr Sharma.

'Madhu and myself occupied a separate wing. Since I am a vegetarian I had a second kitchen. Out of twenty-four hours a day I was spending eight hours with Meena. She was a great friend,' he reminisced.

Kishore Sharma increasingly began to play a vital role in Meena's professional life. He became her constituted attorney and took on all the duties which previously Baqar and Amrohi had handled: signing of contracts, negotiating money, agreeing shooting dates, etc.

Make a note, the third 'landmark' in my heroine's life is Janki Kutir. The five years she lived here were the years in which she fell.

The odd peg of brandy, a minor habit from Rembrandt, increased voluminously; and it was nothing now for my heroine to go through a bottle or more a day. Brandy was her drink and she drank it neat, without ice, without water; and she drank it when she felt like it—which was most of the time. Invariably she sipped alone.

Dharmendra was almost a daily visitor at Janki Kutir. Together they would open a bottle and spend a few hours. These were the good times.

Now there is an impression that Dharam (as she used to call him) was responsible for encouraging her towards the bottle. They say she drank because of him, because he insisted.

Like all good Punjabis, Dharam then and still enjoys his booze; but it is a lie that he persuaded or pressurized Meena to drink. Actually there was no need for that. If anything he was unhappy about her drinking and tried to stop her. He nearly succeeded: while Dharam was around, Meena's imbibing was restricted, once he left it was rampant.

Work, however, did not stop. In 1964, Bimal Roy's *Benazir* was released and so was Kidar Sharma's *Chitralekha*. Other releases included *Ghazal*, *Main Ladki Hun*, *Sanjh Aur Savera*. Alas,

not one of these films including Bimal Roy's effort is worth
analysis or consideration. All that this kind of cinema did for
my heroine was keep her in the public eye.

Again, in the end of 1964 she was to know happiness briefly.
Dharam was everything she wanted then: honest, reliable,
large, loving and comforting.

She saw a lot of him at work and after work. In 1964, my
heroine was involved in five films and in four of these—*Purnima,
Chandan Ka Palna, Phool Aur Patthar, Kaajal*—he was very much
in the scenes.

And with great abandon did she love. Meena, to her eternal
credit, was an honourably honest woman when it came to
the affairs of the heart; and since she truly loved this Punjabi
youth she saw no reason either to be ashamed or to keep it
a secret.

This honesty runs so contrary to the usual practice in the
world Meena was employed that it not only deserves notice but
also commendation. Her colleagues, like her, had lovers, but
they drove in late at night, incognito, wearing dark glasses and
hired rooms in hotels under false names. They were ashamed
of what they were doing. Not my heroine, she was proud.

At cocktail parties, at premieres, Meena openly showered
affection on Dharam. Sometimes she would take his hand
and the next day it would be in print. On one occasion,
mischievously almost, she recited a love couplet from
Ghalib which left no doubt in the audience's mind about Mr
Dharmendra's position in Meena's heart.

In 1964 and 1965, those in the business whose job it
was to report rumour and gossip were not short of material.
Interestingly, on the screen the romantic association wasn't
immediately successful. *Purnima* went away unnoticed, and

Kaajal which was noticed had Dharmendra as second man, with Raaj Kumar taking the main honours. Individually, Meena's performance in *Kaajal* was hailed and it was rumoured that this particular excellence would probably fetch my heroine another award.

It was only in early 1966 that the Dharam-Meena team established itself as a winner through O.P. Ralhan's *Phool Aur Patthar*.

The success of *Phool Aur Patthar* was based on a number of elements complementing each other: good music, advanced photography, arresting titles (a taxi driver told me he had seen the film seven times because of the 'first class' beginning) judicious mixture of breast, bottom and cabaret, and of course flawless Meena Kumari acting coupled with a competent effort by Dharmendra. All in all a shrewdly packaged commercial film. (Ralhan himself had no small part in his venture. He is one of the few natural comics we have, and it is a pity he has gone in for the megaphone instead of the laughs.)

My heroine had never paused to consider the long-term possibilities of her association with Dharam. Really she was not that kind of woman. For her what mattered was the present, and if she could snatch fleeting moments of happiness, it was enough.

In fact, if Meena had paused to consider she would have noticed many difficulties. Mr Dharmendra was a married man. He had a son and a simple homely Punjabi wife, and his allegiance to his family was absolute. Meena was aware of this. Dharam loved her but he wasn't willing to sacrifice his marriage for this love. On her end, Meena was still officially Kamal Amrohi's wife, so she wasn't free either. 'To get married,' she told a friend in 1965, 'you need a "barat". We are both helpless.'

In early May 1966, Bombay's socialites received an invitation: 'The Chairman & Board of Directors of Messrs Bennett Coleman and Company request the pleasure of your company at the Thirteenth Annual Filmfare Awards on Saturday, May 7, 1966 at Shanmukhananda Hall, King's Circle, Bombay at 9.15 p.m.'

Those who were not socialites plagued the *Times of India* offices for invitations. The police band was commissioned; 'printing parking stickers, ensuring plane seats, hotel accommodation and tourist cars for distinguished out-of-town guests' were other headaches to be eased. The orgy of self-congratulation was on in all its vulgar glory.

Reposing calmly in Janki Kutir was the recipient of the Best Actress award. Since she was winning it for the fourth time, Meena Kumari was a bit blase. She had now set a record—a point which most scribes have missed—(no other actress has won more Best Actress awards than my heroine); and although there was a view among the jury that since Meena had won three awards it might be a good idea to encourage somebody else, this view was beaten. (Conscious of the hazards of punditry, I still predict that Meena Kumari will win her fifth award for *Pakeezah* posthumously. And I also predict that for many many years my heroine's achievement in winning awards will remain untouched.)

For once she was not escorted by Chandan. On the platform she sat next to Sunil Dutt and Dilip Kumar and laughed as Tony Randall, a visiting and slightly obscure American comedian, 'had the audience roaring with laughter throughout his speech'. It was Mr Randall who presented 'the woman in white' her fourth award.

On 7 May 1966, Meena Kumari the film actress justifiably

felt that artistically there were no more bridges to cross. Her fame was secure for all time to come.

Despite Dharmendra's affections, Meena Kumari was now a firm addict of the bottle. She was drinking heavily and drinking desperately. One bottle, two bottles, even more.

There is a rumour that she was not always taking brandy. Those who were responsible for purchasing her alcohol kept switching bottles and my heroine, consequently, was receiving all sorts of shoddy illicit liquor (Tharra, etc.). After the first few pegs even connoisseurs can be cheated about what they are drinking, and so was Meena. Additionally, she had reached a stage where she didn't care what she got—as long as she got.

The disease which finally eliminated her was the disease of the liver and this is invariably caused by wholesale consumption of spirits. In the film industry this affliction is particularly popular and its most recent victim was the singer Geeta Dutt (other notable victims being Shailendra, Saigal, Jaikishen).

The strange thing is that my heroine drank seriously for only three years (1965–68), and to get the disease I am talking about in that short period is certainly an achievement, and further, an outright indication of how immoderately Meena was drinking. I am tempted to believe that not only was the quantity of her drinking at fault, but also the quality.

I believe she took her drinks in good faith, hoping them to be genuine. Thus the verdict must be that she was short-changed by her relatives and those supposed to be looking after her. My own view is that Meena knew all about the counterfeit alcohol, but she just didn't care. In fact, by mixing her drinks, she got her nasha quicker, which in turn helped her to run away from reality quicker.

She didn't lose her sense of humour though. Talking to Abrar Alvi, her neighbour and director of *Sahib Bibi Aur Ghulam*, she said, 'It's funny but I think I have become Chhoti Bahu in real life.'

A great film actress has allegiances other than those to liquor. My heroine was also making films, and you may wonder how she could have continued to work if she was sloshed the whole day. Indeed it is a wonder. 'Many mornings when I came to take Meena to the studio she was in no state to come. By eleven in the morning she had gone through one bottle, and I sometimes had to bodily lift her, put her in the car and take her to work. As we came near to the studio I could see a change in her, and when we finally got to the studio she was perfectly sober, with complete command over her faculties. It seemed miraculous but she did this time and time again.' This is the testimony of Kishore Sharma who was now married to Meena's younger sister Madhu and living in Janki Kutir.

By the end of 1966, Mr Dharmendra, a big star now, had disappeared from the scene, and the new man in Meena Kumari's life was a genteel gentleman called Rahul.

I know nothing of Mr Rahul's acting abilities. I also know nothing of his background. He was Meena's most mysterious man. He came and went like this year's monsoon, leaving hardly any trace behind. I have, however, seen one photo of him with Meena and he has what can best be described as an 'innocent face'. He was much younger to Meena and what charms he had for her, only she knows.

It appears they were making some film together (a film which was never completed) and got so friendly that gossip during those days confirmed matrimony. It was reported, even in the press, that like her mother, my heroine had renounced her religion, embraced Arya Samaj and garlanded Mr Rahul in a temple. Others said that the wedding had taken place in a church.

Mr Rahul on his part went around advertising that Meena and he were not married only technically. Otherwise, he said, she was his beloved and would remain so for all time to come. Possibly he was a trifle ambitious.

Very effectively Meena crushed all innuendos. She said Rahul was young enough to be her son. She was fond of him but the question of renouncing her religion and marrying him just did not arise.

I have some complaints and questions to ask of the thirty-odd people living with Meena Kumari in Janki Kutir. Not one of them tried to dissuade her from drinking. If anything, they were oversolicitous and ensured that she was well stocked. I doubt if my heroine would have listened to them but the effort could still have been made.

Shama (Meena's stepsister) was, I believe, supervising affairs, and although there was, and is, much rivalry between sisters and stepsisters, a few things need to be discussed and explained.

Abrar Alvi told me that one night a servant knocked at his house. The servant said he would like to borrow, if possible, some 'pao' (cheap bread). It transpired that my heroine had come back late from work and found there was no food for her. Famished, she sent her servant to her neighbour's house for some food. Alvi says he was amazed at the details of the request. 'She asked for "pao", not meat or eggs. Just plain bread.'

Meena Kumari's relatives were living off her, eating off her, and the least they could do was leave her some dinner.

It is astounding, and a tribute to Meena's professional

perseverance that in the years 1966–67 she was employed in four films. Despite unreliable lovers, despite unreliable alcohol, despite unreliable dinner, despite unreliable friends, she had *Babu Begum*, *Majhli Didi*, *Noor Jehan*, *Abhilasha* in various stages of completion. All of which goes to prove that India's No. 1 tragedienne did not live by bread alone.

Even though the Rahul business lasted no more than a couple of months, those who claimed to be my heroine's friends were distinctly unhappy. They thought her choice was unworthy. Mr Kishore Sharma says he quarrelled with Meena on the Rahul subject and left Janki Kutir.

Meena stayed on, and continued with her drinking. The combination of arduous work, late hours, bad boozing, irregular meals, no exercise had the expected effects. She put on weight, especially round the abdomen, and she was frequently sick.

Sickness was not new to Meena. Ever since she was a child she had to grapple with ill health. 'Medicines have become an integral part of my life,' she wrote in an article. However, this present sickness seemed at once venomous and persistent. Initially she ignored it. 'It is just a fever,' she said. But it wasn't just a fever. Those who could see noticed how large and bulging her stomach had become.

Meena's physician was Dr J.R. Shah and he too was alarmed at the deteriorating state of his patient. Of course, everyone knew the cause: brandy and excess of it.

Shah advised Meena to control, if not eliminate her drinking. She had a special and charming way with requests such as these. She would agree and thank the person for his advice and consideration, promising him that she would do as required. Once he was gone, she would do as she saw fit.

The question is how could she stop drinking. She had, as she saw it, no emotional support; her family life was not exactly ideal; and the possibilities for the future looked extremely grim. In these circumstances she needed a crutch, and for people the world over in her state the bottle has been the most potent, if disastrous, crutch.

Her logic was this: if I am perpetually inebriated, I will be perpetually out of my senses, and I will be perpetually able to avoid thinking of the future. Bertrand Russell would probably find holes in this logic, but if he knew the background he would probably be sympathetic. Dr Shah by now was rightfully suspecting that there was more to my heroine's illness. Later he confirmed that what Meena Kumari was suffering from was 'cirrhosis of the liver'. In layman's language this means that the liver has become defective and is not performing its usual functions. If the liver does not function efficiently, the blood circulation in the body is affected and blood begins to collect in the abdomen.

Everybody wanted Meena to go to a hospital, but she refused. 'Eventually, things got so bad we had to literally throw her into an ambulance. She was kicking and shouting but we just put her in the vehicle,' one of the inmates of Janki Kutir told me.

They took her to a clinic and here she stayed for a few days. She was treated and she partially recovered.

Medical advice, however, was that my heroine needed more advanced and permanent cure. Her liver was in a bad state and if it got aggravated any further, it would become beyond repair. She should go without delay, they all said, to London.

Kishore Sharma was mainly responsible for organizing the mechanics of the London trip. He had, as a law student, lived there previously, and Meena chose him as companion and nurse for her overseas journey.

June is London's prettiest month. The sun shines, men forget to wear their long solemn overcoats, office girls try out their little-worn summer garments, the grass is green, and the normally reserved Englishman smiles, even at strangers, as he says with great pride, 'Lovely day.'

In this season, accompanied by Mr Kishore Sharma, my heroine landed at Heathrow airport, and went straight to the Royal Free Infirmary in Islington North, London. In the infirmary a bed was booked for her and two nurses hired especially at £8 a day.

Her physician in Islington was a lady doctor called Sheila Sherlock, and for two months this doctor submitted my heroine to liver biopsy.

The younger sister Madhu (Mrs Kishore Sharma) made a flying visit to London. She stayed by her sister for fifteen days. Assured that the treatment was going well, she returned.

From the months of June to August, Meena Kumari was in the safe hands of Dr Sherlock. She was responding favourably to the treatment and by August she was looking well recovered.

Not far away from London, in a different country, is a town called Geneva, and this town has made its name because unfriendly world leaders periodically gather here to become less unfriendly. It is also a place where people come to recuperate. The picturesque Alps, the clean country air, the peace and quiet, the easy availability of cheese and chocolate have all made Geneva a favourite with politicians and patients.

Meena Kumari and Kishore Sharma came here too and lived in a hotel called Beau Rivage. 'She was extremely happy.

She loved Geneva and we used to spend a lot of time talking about things past and even her old boyfriends. When it was time to return to India she didn't want to go back,' recollected Kishore Sharma.

The medicines of London and the air of Geneva had a salutary effect on my heroine. When she returned to India in September 1968 she was, to use Mr Sharma's words, 'in the pink of health'. She had become a little slimmer, there was more colour on the countenance and, most importantly, the liver was in much better shape.

On the fifth day of her arrival, Meena Kumari—contrary to doctor's instructions—resumed work. If she wasn't well enough to go to the studio, the studio came to her— shooting for *Abhilasha* took place in Janki Kutir.

In the year 1969 a quietly perceptible but momentous change was coming over Hindi cinema; a change which was to have profound consequences on Meena's career.

Producers in Bombay had long been yearning for sex on the screen. But the social climate (whatever that means) and the Jana Sangh did not permit the debasement of either Indian culture or Indian woman—especially on billboards and posters.

In 1969, however, the attitude towards sex was becoming more permissive. Hippies gloriously celebrated love on the beaches, foreign magazines showed how Western man and woman had decided on salvation through meditation and sex, and above all, European and American cinema, which trickled into this country, became more daring and explicit on libido.

As a result there was a lot of talk in Delhi and Bombay about the restrictions the creative Indian director faced in regard to sex. And people of liberal opinion agreed that if display of intimacy was seriously handled, and if it helped in the development of the creator's conception, it was justified, indeed honourable.

Hypocrisy made its own adjustments to this judgement. There was still no open passionate kissing in the Bombay studios, but a tight embrace and brushing of lips was permissible. There were still no silhouette shots of copulation, but showing the leading man and woman carelessly in bed was permissible.

Simultaneously, a whole new breed of sexy actresses made their debut and were quickly popular. My heroine couldn't compete with Mumtaz, Simi, Rakhee and Hema Malini when it came to 'Hipster' saris.

She was also thirty-six years old, and that is an age in Bombay when they put you to seed. For some unaccountable reason, all story writers in Hindi cinema seem to think that falling in love is the prerogative of the under-twenty-five. Therefore, all romantic plots concern people of that age, and all leading roles go to those who look and act twenty-five. Meena Kumari did not look and act that age (thank God for that) and this was another reason why she was having difficulties securing the kind of contracts she was securing before. If you examine the films my heroine made between 1969 and 1972 (more than six), you will find only one in which she had the lead.

So they made her play an old woman, an elder sister, a widowed wife. Directors and people who knew her say that she took this fall philosophically. 'She was not worried about these things,' Gulzar said.

I disagree with Gulzar. I don't think she took the fall philosophically. She knew, and rightly, that she still had a lot of life as an actress left, and she also knew that the new crop of actresses were amateurs in front of her.

Meena made no noise publicly. In fact, characteristically, the transition was graceful. And even to third-rate roles she gave her best. In *Jawab*, *Dushman*, *Gomti Ke Kinare* she is par excellence.

Did she drink after London? Some say yes, some say no. I am told Dr Sherlock had warned my heroine before she left the infirmary, 'The day you want to die have a drink.'

I think the message had got through. Meena understood that the bottle would be lethal for her and she stayed away. Sawan Kumar Tak, the last man in her life, told me, 'Not only did she not drink, she wouldn't let me drink either. She did not touch a drop after returning from London.' I tend to agree with that.

By the end of 1969 my heroine couldn't take Janki Kutir any more. She quarrelled with her relatives and decided that she would live by herself. Again Mr Sharma was instructed to look for a place.

The fourth landmark in my heroine's life is 'Landmark'. In Carter Road, Bandra, on the eleventh floor of a building called Landmark, Mr Sharma purchased on Meena's behalf her first home. Till now she had lived either in alien or rented property.

She couldn't live alone. Khursheed, the eldest sister, was summoned and she moved in with her children. This time the people living with Meena were few, and for herself she built a special bedroom. In consultation with Kishore Sharma, she decorated Landmark to her heart's desire.

I was privileged to spend a few minutes in her bedroom. It was an unnerving and eerie experience. I saw her large bed made up, I saw her books (Alistair MacLean, Gulshan Nanda, Emily Bronte), I saw her sea stones, I saw her gods in the little mandir she had built in her bedroom, and all the time I kept telling myself, remember India's greatest actress lived here.

This room, resplendent with all her whims and fancies, became her hideout. Most of the time she spent by herself either writing her diary or reading. Work was scarce and I suspect she didn't want any.

After her fall, my heroine was involved in only two decent films—*Pakeezah*, *Mere Apne*.

Mere Apne was directed by her old friend Gulzar and in his film she came a full circle—she wasn't playing the elder sister any more but a full-fledged old woman. Gulzar's film was a remake of Tapan Sinha's Bengali film *Apanjan* and, if nothing else, he tackled a bold and purposeful theme: youth unrest. And the predominant opinion is that Mr Gulzar's directorial debut was promising. Certainly my heroine felt so. She went around telling her friends, 'You must see *Mere Apne*.'

Meanwhile, her own performance was reviewed ravingly: 'As the old woman Meena Kumari merits kudos. She brings a lump to the throat and makes for first departure towards character acting highly rewarding and memorable.'

The penultimate year of her life was spent mostly in bed or in the hospital. The fever just wouldn't leave her and if she wasn't sick in Landmark, she was sick in St Elizabeth's Nursing Home.

Only one unfinished film remained, *Gomti Ke Kinare*, and she was getting restless. She warned its maker to get it over with quickly. She said she wasn't sure how long she would be around. Finally, on 29 December, she went to the studio for the last time and finished the film. Professional work was complete.

On 31 December 1971, she had an ex-lover for a visitor. Dharam came unannounced just before midnight, and together they reminisced quietly and ushered in the new year. He left after a few minutes, and she tried to get some sleep totally oblivious that the world round her was ringing out the old and ringing in the new. The year 1972 was going to be a short one for her.

FIVE

Pakeezah

First Meena Kumari made this film with her money. Then with her death.

– Mr Habib Khan
(taxi driver)

They thought he was mad. To find locations that matched his script he travelled the length and breadth of the country. So extensive and far-reaching were his journeys that they became a joke. Someone remarked that a more appropriate name for this film would be 'India trip'. Not deterred by ridicule he continued his discoveries and to obtain jewellery he travelled first to Benares, then to Jaipur, and then to Trivandrum. He found what he went looking for.

In quest of a 'kabrastan', the man of these travels, Kamal Amrohi, landed at the Chambal river. Here he discovered precisely the spot of his choice. Situated correctly on a height, this cemetery was just what Kamal had in mind. He liked the location immensely but he was in two minds. Supposing he selected this unbelievable strange-looking place, would there be a danger that the audience would think it a fake, erected in a studio? Not wanting to take this risk, he abandoned what was otherwise an ideal site. I bring this up just to indicate the sort of pains Mr Amrohi took to ensure realism.

Much much earlier, on 18 January 1958, there had been an unostentatious mahurat. Sitting on the ground, Kamal and Meena had folded their hands and asked for blessings for a new film. It was then called *Pakeezah* (the name has a fascinating history too. It was changed many times due to superstitious reasons, but finally the original stayed), and at that time it was envisaged in CinemaScope and black-and-white.

After the failure of *Daera*, *Pakeezah* as an idea was roaming Amrohi's mind. The concept, he says, was irretrievably fixed with his love for his wife. He hoped to create a film which would be worthy of her as an actress, and worthy of the love he felt for her as a woman. Thus the creation had only one central character and around the fortunes of this character the fate of the film revolved.

Kamal declares that every line he wrote he had Meena in mind. He wished to present her on the screen as no one had before: beautiful, sad, sanguine, dejected, calculating, sexy, he ambitioned to capture as many dimensions of her as he knew of. 'Shah Jahan made Taj Mahal for his wife,' said Amrohi's PR man, 'Kamal Sahab wanted to do the same with *Pakeezah*.'

In their chambers they talked about it. He read her the lines, asked for her opinions and found she was usually in full agreement with the direction of the story.

What both Amrohi and my heroine had fallen for was the idea of the 'nautch girl'.

As a starting point the idea was superbly seductive. Although before Mr Amrohi, scores of film-makers had attempted something similar, they had all trivialized it, vulgarized it, commercialized it. A treatment which blended the aesthetic with the authentic was lacking. There was much fertile material lurking around the life of a dancing girl and most of it had been untouched.

By 1960 he had written every line of the script. From the titles to the last frame all was on paper. It is characteristic of the way Kamal works that not many commas or full stops or words were added to the script. The 1960 idea on paper can be seen unchanged on the screen in 1972.

Despite the fact that Amrohi wished to make a realistic, unvulgarized film, he was ambitious. He saw in *Pakeezah* an epic, a larger-than-life film with hundreds of extras, with expensive and exotic sets, with superhuman effort made to preserve period flavour, and all this he wished to do with the collected professional proficiency he had acquired in nearly two decades. This was no do-it-yourself cinema, instead, it was visioned as the ultimate in spectacle and pageantry.

I suspect Amrohi set himself a standard to beat. K. Asif had earlier made *Mughal-e-Azam* (Kamal had written most of the dialogue) and Amrohi was determined to cross Mr Asif's effort as far as grandeur and visual craft were concerned. If Asif had memorable battle scenes, Amrohi would have memorable dancing scenes. If Asif had a memorable historical plot, Amrohi would have a memorable human plot. This rivalry existed in real life too, and its antecedents went back to the days when Mr Amrohi was thinking of *Anarkali*. I have a feeling that he always felt that his interpretation of this love story, had it been completed, would have been better than Asif's *Mughal-e-Azam*.

Legitimately, you might ask why I devote a separate chapter, the only separate chapter, to a Meena Kumari film. The reason is this: of all the seventy-seven movies my heroine made, she had a special niche for *Pakeezah*. My own view is that she was wrong; that Sahebjan was not her most gripping performance. However, intellectually and emotionally, of all the films she made, *Pakeezah* held her most.

Kamal Amrohi's blurb for his film explains this best: 'For her to fall in love was forbidden—it was a sin she was told. A nautch girl is born to delight others, such is her destiny. She preferred to die a thousand deaths than to live as a body without a soul. And yet when her restless soul could not suppress this surging desire to love and be loved, she took birth as Kamal Amrohi's *Pakeezah*.'

You are right if you consider 90 per cent of this blurb as overwritten rhetoric. There is however one sentence worth considering: 'the surging desire to love and be loved'. And it was this line in which Meena saw a reflection of her life. She too, she felt, was born with a surging desire to love and be loved. It seemed to her that the story of the nautch girl was her story, and really on the screen there was no need to act.

In 1961, when the camera was set in motion, the following had been signed: Josef Wirsching as photographer, Ghulam Mohammed as music director, Ashok Kumar as the hero, Meena Kumari as the heroine, and a handful of Urdu writers as lyricists. Subsequently, only one change was made and that concerned Mr Ashok Kumar.

Of all the artistes, the speediest was Mr Ghulam Mohammed, the music director. Before the camera was set in motion for the first time, he had the entire music for the film ready and waiting. The music that is on top of the 'Binaca Hit Parade' today was written a decade ago.

Between 1961 and 1964 work continued unabated on *Pakeezah*, but there were problems. Even with unabated work the number of feet in the can was small. There were many reasons for this.

Meena was a busy and fully booked star in 1961 and although she tried her best she could only squeeze a few days each month for her husband. The husband on his part was not disposed to hurry. *Pakeezah* was his labour of love and he was such a stickler for exactness that the few days he got were invariably spent in getting things right. 'If Mr Amrohi has something in mind, he will continue until he gets what he wants, no matter how long it takes,' Mobin Ansari of Mahal Pictures explained to me.

The progress and culmination of *Pakeezah* was entrenched in the hands of two individuals: Meena Kumari and Kamal Amrohi—the others were expendable and could be substituted. Consequently, the personal relationship of these two people was vital in the continuing progress of this film. If the relationship was bad, progress was slow. If the relationship was good, progress was fast.

At the very outset, the film was commenced at a time when Meena Kumari's marriage was breathing its last. And my heroine knew that her husband had put all his eggs in one basket, i.e., *Pakeezah*. She also knew she was indispensable to this film, the maker having himself pronounced, '*Pakeezah* is Meena Kumari.'

By early 1964 some work was complete. However, in these three years a terrific amount of money (Rs 40 lakh) had been spent, mostly in erecting and perfecting the many expensive sets. Therefore, when Meena's departure from the Amrohi house was imminent, Kamal was faced with a perplexing problem. He couldn't be entirely certain that Meena would continue to work in his film after she left him. The thought of scrapping what he had completed and starting afresh with a new heroine was too drastic to contemplate and perhaps impractical. To begin with, he had invested all he had, and without Meena in the credits he would have an impossible task raising money in the market.

Baqar, Mr Amrohi's secretary, states that a few days prior to my heroine leaving Rembrandt he made her a proposition: 'I know you are unhappy here and want to leave. I shall help you to leave. In fact I will find you a house where you can live independently. I only want one promise from you, that you will finish *Pakeezah*.'

After she actually left, my heroine repeatedly confirmed that only her personal association with Amrohi was severed. She was still available as a film star to him, if he desired.

But so much bad feeling had been engendered during the separation that for a few months after, work automatically came to a stop. Amrohi says that he came to a stage where he thought of abandoning the film. Since he had conceived it as a tribute to his wife and since his wife was no longer by his side the raison d'être of the film had disappeared. *Pakeezah* was a work of love and a man with a broken heart was not qualified to pursue it.

In 1964, Meena was still right on top. Her assignment book was full and her private life was miserable. She had little time to think of the worries of her Pali Hill husband reportedly in mourning over her.

A year it took for Kamal to regain his equanimity, and then he again seriously began thinking of *Pakeezah*. The film script which he had shelved for a year or so was dusted, and he reassembled his resources.

The important query was: who was going to approach Meena? Amrohi was too proud a man to go begging to his wife, and he made approaches to Meena through intermediaries, asking her to resume work. My heroine was suitably non-committal. She neither said yes nor no.

Chandan religiously visited her each Eid and gave her 'Iddi', but he never once raised the subject of *Pakeezah*. I am sure he wanted to.

In moments of desperation, Kamal thought of a substitute for my heroine. He even made some sort of search, but each time he came back from where he had started. The one and only woman who could play Sahebjan was Manju.

From 1958 onwards Ashok Kumar was getting no younger. If in the late 1950s he still found main parts, they were now very scarce. Ashok Kumar had graduated mostly to elder brother roles and Kamal Amrohi was confronted with another difficulty. He had to find a younger leading man for his film.

Among the multitude *Pakeezah* humours, one concerns the hero. *Filmfare* joked that Amrohi changed his heroes 'like his shirts'. I don't know how many shirts Mr Amrohi has, but it is true that the part of the forest officer in his film was thrown around.

Those who were in and out of the running included Rajendra Kumar, Sunil Dutt, Dharmendra and Raaj Kumar.

Mr Dharmendra nearly got it. Amrohi was greatly impressed by this young man, and physically Dharam had all the attributes necessary for one who lives and looks after a jungle.

However, when Dharam's association with my heroine started swelling, someone warned him that if he got too friendly with Meena his chances of landing the coveted role would be jeopardized. He paid no heed, and so it came to pass. 'Although he (Kamal) thought Dharmendra entirely fit for the role, he withdrew the offer. He couldn't work with a man who was publicly having an affair with his wife,' an Amrohi aide told me.

Raaj Kumar and Amrohi had worked previously together in *Dil Apna Aur Preet Parayi*, and the one thing that Kamal liked about Raaj Kumar was his voice. Not only did he speak literate Hindustani, he spoke it well and deep.

Mr Raaj Kumar had his own doubts. 'At first I was inclined to turn down the role for the simple reason that it had gone the rounds to certain other actors and landed back in the creator Kamal Amrohi's lap.' Eventually he agreed. He says he thought the role to be challenging, and the pleasure of working under Kamal Amrohi was also a reason.

Time moved on but *Pakeezah* didn't. On 25 August 1968, Mr Amrohi wrote a letter to his estranged wife, '... only *Pakeezah's* completion remains unsettled. You have made a condition that unless I give you a divorce you will not complete *Pakeezah*. Even this knot can be untied ... I will free you from your marital ties. After this if you wish to help complete "your *Pakeezah*", I would be most happy to do so. This is my request, that *Pakeezah* on which the fortune of many people depends, and which has the good wishes of so many people should not be left uncompleted if possible.' The next few lines of this letter are particularly poignant and humble. 'You have better means. You have power. You have box-office appeal, and most of all *Pakeezah* needs you personally ... *Pakeezah* that is like a sinking ship will reach ashore under your care.'

Kamal Amrohi would not have written this kind of letter unless he was without options—and in 1968 he was. Somehow Meena Kumari had to be persuaded to resume work.

Amrohi was fortunate in as much that in 1968 things for Meena Kumari, the film star, were not going too well. Her greatest problem lay in securing leading roles. Like Ashok Kumar, in 1968 she had fallen to elder sister roles. Very few wanted her to play the romantic lead.

This situation was further exacerbated by my heroine's poor health. Word had spread inside the industry that Meena Kumari was suffering physically and this deterred those thinking of signing her on in a big way. In the year 1968 not only did Kamal Amrohi need Meena Kumari, Meena Kumari needed Kamal Amrohi—since he was the one man offering her a comeback as a leading lady.

Nargis argues that she was instrumental in restarting Amrohi's unfinished film. Sunil Dutt also says he has a share. It appears Nargis asked Meena if she would complete Kamal Amrohi's film. Meena said yes.

I do not wish to take credit away from Mrs Dutt, but I suspect my heroine had already made up her mind. Mr and Mrs Dutt were helpful in conveying messages. Nothing, I feel, more than that.

On 16 March 1969, five years and twelve days after she had left her husband, Meena Kumari reported for work again on *Pakeezah*. Kamal organized a great reception. He gave his wife a peda (sweet) as a peace offering, and made a documentary film of her arrival at the studio.

From March 1969 to December 1971, Amrohi and my heroine worked and worked and worked. The last three years were years of feverish activity. Meena now had time on her hands and she willingly gave any dates that her husband required.

Every film, I suppose, has incidents behind it. So has Amrohi's *Pakeezah*.

On outdoor shooting, Mr Amrohi's unit travelled in two cars, and these cars were poised in the direction of Delhi. Near a place called Shivpuri in MP, the cars all but ran out of petrol. There were just a few trickles left and for miles around there was nothing except a long, deserted, straight road. It was discovered that a bus passed on this route every morning from which fuel could be purchased. 'Good,' said Amrohi, 'we'll spend the night here.'

He said this without knowing that he was in the thick of India's most notorious dacoit area. Mr Jayaprakash Narayan had not yet started his mission to reform the criminals and these dacoits were reported to be both ferocious and heartless. On learning where his cars had halted, he ordered that his unit roll up the windows of the cars and hope for the best.

A little after midnight the occupants of the vehicles were disturbed. They were surrounded by a dozen men. The men knocked on the closed windows and forced their way in. They said they were taking the cars to the police station. The unit did not believe this, but the men were armed and as Mr Mao has taught, all persuasion comes from the barrel of a gun.

The cars were led into a gate. There the occupants were ordered to get out. My heroine, already unwell, was in bad shape. She thought the dacoits meant bodily harm. Mr Amrohi, however, refused to get out of the car. Whoever wanted to meet him could come here, he said.

A few minutes later a young man wearing a silk pyjama and a silk shirt appeared.

'Who are you?' he asked.

'I am Kamal,' Mr Amrohi replied, 'we are on a shooting assignment. We ran out of petrol and are stranded.'

The dacoit thought shooting meant rifle shooting and Amrohi had to explain that they were film shooters. This relieved the dacoit and when he learned that one of the persons in the car was my heroine, his attitude completely changed.

Even dacoits, on their day off, see films, and so did this

robber. He turned out to be a Meena Kumari fan and welcomed his guests in true fan tradition. He organized music, dancing, and food. He provided place to sleep. He instructed his juniors the next morning to fetch petrol for the unit.

From my heroine he wanted a special favour. He sharpened his knife and took it to her. 'Please autograph my hand with this,' he requested. Meena was not new to signing autographs but she had never attempted anything as ambitious as a knife.

Nervously, she wrote her name on this man's hand. He said he was grateful for this favour.

Once the unit left, they found at the next town that they had spent the night in the camp of Madhya Pradesh's renowned and dangerous dacoit—Amrit Lal.

Snakes, bureaucracy, quicksand were other difficulties that Amrohi had to contend with. However, he was determined to shoot at only those places which harmonized with his conception and his script.

By November 1971, the entire film was in the can and the only work left was in the cutting room.

What had happened to the people involved in this film between 1958 and 1972? Some had grown old, some had voluntarily quit, some had retired, some had died.

Two conspicuous deaths were those of Ghulam Mohammed and Josef Wirsching.

Mr Ghulam Mohammed died a pitiable and harrowing death. In the mid-1960s the room for genuine Indian music had virtually disappeared in Hindi films. Cheap imitations of rock 'n' roll were in vogue and the 'Yahoo' type of melody reigned supreme. Ghulam Mohammed was a classical musician. To him 'Yahoo' was anathema and he continued to practise his type of music. Amrohi, recognizing talent, had signed him on but nobody else. Borrowing a tape recorder, Mr Mohammed made rounds to the producers. He played them his *Pakeezah* songs. 'This is the quality of my music,' he would say and ask for work.

The producers were unimpressed. This was no music, they said. This was out of date. Could he produce something more contemporary, more jazzy? Poor Ghulam Mohammed would return with his tape recorder.

In 1968 he was sick. He had no money to buy food. He had no money to buy medicines. Soon, Ghulam Mohammed was dead, unmourned and unremembered. He had died in sickness and in poverty and in shame. Next year, when they are distributing the Filmfare Awards and Ghulam Mohammed gets his for *Pakeezah*, as I confidently expect him to, he will take little comfort in posthumous glory.

The exact temperature of the Manju-Chandan relations after the restarting of *Pakeezah* is, predictably, inexact and open to dispute. A purely working relationship, or was a reconciliation reached?

According to Amrohi, he and Manju had come very close indeed. During the shooting journeys she cared after Chandan as a wife looks after her husband. On his part he says he ensured that Manju was provided all material comforts and conveniences. 'Only physically we were not man and wife. Otherwise in every sense we lived like man and wife,' Amrohi informed me.

Meena, Amrohi says, had by now realized the disastrous folly she had committed by leaving his house. One evening when they were alone she cried bitterly and regretfully. 'Chandan, I can never forgive the people who broke up our marriage,' she said. Such close emotional proximity existed between the two in 1970 that it was suggested Meena go back with her husband to live in Rembrandt. Mr Amrohi, although in favour of this move, felt that Rembrandt may revive painful old memories, and in Meena's delicate health, this could prove to be fatal.

'It was just work between them,' Khursheed told me. 'Meena had no feeling left for Kamal and if he thinks anything else he is fooling himself. How could she feel anything for him after the way he treated her during the shooting of *Pakeezah*.'

Complaints pertaining to lack of proper food, proper medical attention, proper staying arrangements have been made. They say he made her run down a hill twenty-six times for the purposes of a sequence (this complaint I know is false), they say he wouldn't get her the tablets and pills she needed.

I personally don't think my heroine had a major change of heart about her husband. This is borne out by her subsequent attitude to him and by the stipulations in her will. (Mr Amrohi's name in this document is conspicuously absent.)

About February 1972, *Pakeezah* was very much in Bombay's air. The populace was wondering if this heralded and much-talked-about film would live up to its great expectations. *The Illustrated Weekly* in its 30 January issue headlined: 'Meena Kumari's supreme test'. There seemed to be some doubt whether my heroine in her advanced age could do justice to a part which was reported to be grilling and grinding.

On 3 February, in the Arabian Sea a 'Pakeezah Boat' was sailing and in Maratha Mandir the premiere was scheduled. A one-and-a-half-crore rupee film, CinemaScope, Eastmancolor, fifteen years in the making, was at last to be screened.

Looking reflective and refined, my heroine arrived to attend the last premiere of her life. She let Mr Raaj Kumar, for the benefit of the press, kiss her hand and then she went in to see the film.

The next morning reaction was discouraging. The *Times of India* in an unflattering review called *Pakeezah* a 'lavish waste'. Later, the resident critic of *Filmfare*, Mr Banaji, gave it one lonely star (this rating means very poor). Most of the so-called sophisticated critics of India had no time for the hackneyed story of a dancing girl.

My heroine, however, silenced the sceptics. At the age of forty, she had come roaring back to form and demonstrated that she was still in a class of her own. Sahebjan had come out with flying colours; Sahebjan's creator with not so flying.

The Urdu press, more in sympathy with the concept, was fulsome in its praise. They called Mr Amrohi's effort sensitive, historic, moving, beautiful ...

Pakeezah's greatest fan was no other than *Pakeezah*'s heroine. 'I have lived with *Pakeezah* almost as long as I have lived with its creator ... to Meena Kumari *Pakeezah* means a performance. A great performance? That is not for me to say: that is for the people to decide. For me to say is this: it is a performance to deliver which I have, as an actress, had to delve deeper into the secret wells of being than any actor or actress normally delves in the process of his or her professional work.'

As she confesses, she lived with *Pakeezah*, she saw its fortunes rise and fall, and she was followed by this film wherever she went. Both Amrohi and Meena just had to get *Pakeezah* out of their respective systems.

This was also the biggest film of her career, and additionally she saw its story, as I mentioned earlier, as a reflection of her private aspirations. In a way in real life she was a nautch girl.

People came to her for their quota of pleasure and departed. No one cared for her as a person. A film which crystallized this theme was ordained to attract and stay with her.

Meena Kumari's Sahebjan is not my favourite. I don't know why, I saw only competence in this part and not genius. While she was dancing, I would have preferred more lust. While she was playful, I would have preferred more frivolity. While she was briefly happy, I would have preferred more joy. While she was resigned, I would have preferred more fatalism.

I suspect, however, that long after she is dead and gone, millions in India will remember my heroine as the woman who danced and sang 'Inhi Logon Ne'.

Raging controversy exists as to who is the true owner of *Pakeezah*. There is a large body which says that without Meena Kumari this film is nothing. Mr Habib Khan, the taxi driver whom I have quoted in the beginning, echoed the thoughts of many people who had seen this film.

Let me make my own position on *Pakeezah* clear. I thought it was a flawed but noble attempt. No one before Amrohi had captured honestly the dilemma of the dancing girl. Certainly many debased and unworthy commercial formulas were used. Certainly the story was unoriginal, and all that bit about the train stopping inches away from the heroine could have been avoided. But what makes this long-awaited film worthwhile is its devotion, its period authenticity. I don't think I have seen any other film which evokes a strata of Muslim society with more correctness and realism than *Pakeezah*.

Of course the difficulty is that Amrohi's is a minority film. Mr Banaji, the very worthy critic of *Filmfare*, and other worthy critics dabbling in Pasolini and Renoir are disqualified from comment. If you have no sympathy with Muslim folklore and if you can't speak and understand Hindustani, you might as well not see *Pakeezah*. When one nautch girl says to another, '*Sahebjan ham ko ek din ke liye apni kismet de do*,' the nuances of this request can only be relished by someone who comprehends the language, and by someone who has been to the 'kotha' of a dancing girl himself.

I don't think *Pakeezah* is a great film. But compared to the likes of *Hare Rama Hare Krishna* it is a classic.

Nostalgia as a box-office ingredient is new. Those who do not like Amrohi say that this film is only running because of Meena's timely death. The crowds outside Maratha Mandir and scores of other cinemas all over the country are crowds of reverence. These people have not come to see *Pakeezah*, they have come to pay respects to Meena Kumari.

Amrohi denies this. His film, he feels, is gathering crowds entirely on merit. Although I somewhat agree with him, I feel a small percentage of the crowd is possibly on a pilgrimage. The major percentage is there to see Mr Amrohi's wizardry. No film can run house-full for thirty-three weeks, as it is today, on nostalgia alone.

This still does not answer the question, whose film?

I think you have to be some sort of pervert to deny Kamal Amrohi his right to this film. He used my heroine at an age when she was lost, he used for his leading man an actor who was no Rajesh Khanna, he took for a music director someone who was in disgrace and unemployed—and from this he produced one of the greatest hits in recent times.

My heroine herself acknowledged Kamal's ownership. '*Pakeezah* is the beloved which has been born of this film-maker's imagination nearly two decades ago. *Pakeezah* is the vision

which has haunted his soul for as long as I can remember.'
Ashok Kumar made the same point, a little more openly,
'Actually and literally *Pakeezah* is Kamal Amrohi, and Kamal
Amrohi alone. Every frame of it, every motivation, every
plot-curve, every character in it, is exactly as its visualizer
conceived.'

Good, bad, or indifferent, it is monstrous that we should
take one film away from a man who has made only three in
his life.

Six

Death

Appa! Appa! I don't want to die.

— Meena Kumari
(*to Khursheed from her deathbed*)

On 24 March 1972, the three Ali Bux daughters were busy playing cards at their flat in Bandra. The game was going well for Meena. She was winning quickly. Khursheed was planning her moves while Madhu appeared in deep thought.

'My God!' exclaimed my heroine, 'by the time you two play your hand I will be dead.'

'Munna, I don't like you talking about dying all the time. Why, if anybody is going to die around here it is going to be me. After all I am the eldest,' said Khursheed.

'No, no,' came in Madhu, 'I want to die first. Yes, I want to die. As the youngest it is my duty to die first.'

'Both of you have families, children to bring up. You have responsibilities. How can you die? I have no one. And remember, I am the one who has a kafan from Mecca.'

With this statement, Meena put an end to all speculation and request for first demise. She decided that she would be off first.

In deference to her decision, two weeks earlier she had had another one of her attacks. As usual, parts of her body—the legs and hands—became immobile due to painful swelling. Most of the day and night she was bedridden, and even on the bed she found it impossible to stretch out (the prostrate position with a swollen body is uncomfortable). Consequently, she sat up in bed with the aid of large pillows behind her back, and in this very state managed a sort of sleep. Nirmal, the faithful ayah/companion, did exemplary and ceaseless work in easing my heroine's pain. Mr Shabd Kumar of *Film Industry*, who was working on a biography of my heroine then, went to see her. He reported, 'On Saturday—the last Saturday of her life—when I had met Meenaji at her residence, her condition was quite serious and painful. Although her face was quite normal and pleasing, her abdomen was excessively bloated with water. I was finding it very difficult to see her suffering when a mild shriek of pain passed from her lips and looking at me, she remarked, *"Cheekhne mein sharam aati hai"* (I am ashamed of shrieking).'

25 March. The patient worsened. The attacks of discomfort became successively more frequent and she lost all use of hands and legs. The smallest movement produced excruciating pain. A brave, courageous and experienced woman when it came to physical suffering, my heroine could no longer keep the torment hidden. She told Khursheed of her agony.

Praying and hoping that it would pass, the sister continued with prescribed formulations. In her sickness, Meena had demonstrated a strange kind of resilience. A two- or three-day attack would wilt away and she would be moderately fit again; and so this unhappy cycle had continued in the past. This time, however, the cycle stopped halfway.

On the night of 25 March, Khursheed and Meena had a long serious talk. 'The time has come Appa,' Meena said, 'and perhaps it is the right time. I have no unfinished commitments. Kamal Sahib's *Pakeezah* is finished, Premji's *Dushman* is finished, Sawan's *Gomti Ke Kinare* is finished. No one will be able to say Meena left without completing her work. As far as I could, I have left something for you and your children. Now it is up to you to ensure that they get all the right opportunities. I am ready to die.'

The night she made this announcement was bad for her. She was uncommonly restless and the oxygen cylinder in the bedroom had to be utilized to enable her to breathe peacefully. Further, the first symptoms of deliriousness indicated themselves. Meena kept hitting her hand periodically on the bed with some force. It was a disturbing sight.

26 March. Dr Shah was summoned and Khursheed also rang up Mr Amrohi.

Both arrived almost simultaneously and while Mr Amrohi waited inside the sitting room, Dr Shah examined my heroine. He came out and said that Meena's condition was pretty serious. He would, he said, like a second opinion. Was it acceptable to Amrohi and Khursheed if he sent for Dr Modi? Naturally, they agreed and Amrohi requested the doctor to take all measures necessary for making Meena well again.

Dr Shah and Dr Modi came together on the morning of 27 March, and they were agreed in their diagnosis. My heroine's condition was serious and it was high priority that she be admitted to a hospital where advanced medical facilities existed, and where emergencies could be suitably handled.

Meena was informed of the doctor's decision, but she was undecided. Was it really necessary for her to go? Couldn't the doctors treat her at home? Dr Shah explained to Khursheed as he left that Meenaji's condition was such that if she wanted to live, she would have to go to the hospital. He told her to persuade Meena while he would make arrangements for a room at St Elizabeth's Nursing Home in Malabar Hill.

My heroine's unwillingness to enter a hospital was based on sound prejudice. All her life she had spent in and out of clinics, and she hated them. If death was inevitable now she would like it in her home in Bandra.

Yet, once again she was persuaded. She agreed to her doctor's orders. And perhaps by now she appreciated the seriousness of her condition. She had not eaten anything since the morning and her diet which consisted entirely of fruit juice and glucose lay untouched on the table next to her bed. 'We'll go to the hospital tomorrow,' she told Khursheed.

Strangely, she had a comparatively restful night, and when Dr Shah arrived in the morning he was pleased at the state of his patient. However, the move to the hospital was still on.

28 March, 10 a.m. My heroine summoned her elder sister. 'How much money have we got?' she asked. A quick count and Khursheed answered, 'Hundred rupees.' Meena pondered. How could she be admitted to Bombay's most expensive nursing home with that kind of amount? Clearly, money had to be got, and got quickly.

While these monetary matters were being organized, the doctor came in and enquired the reason for the delay. 'Please get ready quickly. There is no time to waste. I have sent for the ambulance.'

But how could Meena go. The woman who had literally

thrown away lakhs of rupees was today unable to raise hospital fees—such is the transience of wealth.

There was a man my heroine knew rather well who was loaded. He had recently made a film in which she had played the title role, and which was minting money. A nudge and he would send currency. But that man was Kamal Amrohi and that was the last man Meena wished to borrow from. (Mr Amrohi told me he had heard of Meena's financial difficulties and when he went to see her on 28 March he carried a large sum of money in his briefcase in case Meena asked, or in case there was any money shortage.)

When I asked someone close to Meena why she did not touch her husband for a loan, I was told, 'How could she. She had built Amrohi with her own money. What a blow it would have been for her own ego to ask that man for a loan.'

Premji was one of the producers Meena had worked for and Meena suggested to Khursheed that she telephone him. Some money was due from Mr Premji and my heroine was only asking for what was rightfully hers.

Khursheed made the call and came back with good news. Premji promised to send the money as fast as possible.

Relieved, Meena dressed herself in the characteristic sari colour. She sat in front of her dressing table and for the last time ran her thick, black comb through her luscious black hair. 'I will not be coming back this time,' she told Khursheed. 'Here are the keys to my room. Please lock it after I have gone.' Khursheed made a few reassuring sounds. In reply my heroine said, 'After I die I want you to bring my body up to Landmark and from here you must take me and bury me next to Majee and Babujee.'

The bell rang at the door. A messenger had arrived carrying a packet for my heroine. He said he had come from Premji

Sahab. On opening it, Meena found 10,000 rupees. She divided the money into equal parts. Half she gave to her doctor and half to Khursheed.

All was ready for the journey, but before she left she went through farewell rounds. To the relatives, who on hearing the news had gathered in strength, she said adieu and a particularly fond farewell was reserved for Pinky—Khursheed's youngest daughter. My heroine embraced her favourite niece and wished 'Khuda Hafiz'. The little girl burst out crying.

Khursheed helped Meena stand up. She had a parting look at the room she had lived in for three years, the room which had so many of her mementoes—sea-stones, flowers, paintings and of course the books—and which had become her sanctuary.

Walking out of her flat she gave Khursheed one instruction. 'Don't tell Kamal Sahab I have gone to the hospital.'

Getting into the lift she said namaste to the lift man. He was so overcome by this greeting that instead of replying he started crying gently. Downstairs, she did the same thing to the Gorkha watchman who, observing his compatriot, the liftman, joined in the tears.

Meanwhile, the news had spread around Carter Road and a 100-strong crowd had collected near the waiting ambulance. Silently the fans said goodbye and watched the woman they had seen playing a thousand memorable parts, enter the medical vehicle.

One fan, however, was busy with her duties, and when she learnt she came rushing down and caught my heroine a minute before departure. This was the *bhangan* (sweeper woman) and she stood in front of Meena, head bowed, offering her tribute. My heroine, who always carried loose change and some paper notes in a small embroidered bag, gave this woman not only the money but the bag too.

28 March, 11.15 a.m. The ambulance and Meena left Landmark. Inside the ambulance sat Madhu and Khursheed, and in between sat Meena. Opposite were the two brothers-in-law, Mr Altaf and Mr Sharma.

It was an uncomfortable journey. My heroine passed it sometimes resting her head on Madhu's shoulder and sometimes on Khursheed's, and in this state Meena Kumari arrived at the nursing home in Malabar Hill.

It was just after noon when Meena Kumari's ambulance, winding its way through Napean Sea Road, got inside St Elizabeth's Nursing Home. As she must have observed on her many visits, this Home appears more like a three- or four-star luxury hotel than a hospital. Compact, neat with some suggestion of a garden, and Christianity writ large on its face, St Elizabeth's is a modern-looking three-storey mission hospital staffed mainly by Irish, Goan and Parsee sisters.

On the second floor, for Rs 65 a day, Dr Shah hired for his patient, with great difficulty (booking in the Home is very heavy), air-conditioned accommodation. A long clinically clean alley houses private rooms on each side, and each floor has its separate telephone and sister on the desk. Outside the alley is a lobby decorated with a sofa set and table. It is all very friendly and intimate and scarcely an air of death or pain or medicine pervades.

As you enter, the third room on the left is Room 26. It has an armchair, a black blanket, a typical hospital bed and one window which has no view to offer. A push-button mechanism exists, and if you push it, a red bulb entwined by a clinging plant lights up. Room 26 was my heroine's room.

After completion of formalities she was admitted, and the first thing she enquired after was the eating arrangements for her relatives who had accompanied her. 'You have not had any lunch,' she told her sisters and immediately commanded Khursheed that she go down and organize the messing.

Khursheed went down and organized as ordered and also telephoned Mr Amrohi. He said he was going to the studio then but promised to come in the evening.

The doctors in the meantime had got to work on my heroine and had removed three bucketfuls of fluid which had accumulated in her abdomen, and which were causing all the pain. (A cirrhosis patient in fact has little hope but to go to the hospital periodically for fluid removal.) The water pumped out, she was relieved, and when Khursheed came back she was delighted to see her sister sitting up and smiling. 'I am feeling much better,' she said.

Mr Amrohi and son arrived around five o'clock, and he quietly came and sat by his wife's bedside. It was like old times again. Many years ago in a hospital they had held hands and looked into each other's eyes; today they were holding hands again, but in the many intervening years, love had turned sour and now there was just pity and perhaps regret. The only lines appropriate were lines from Fitzgerald: 'O love! if you and I with fate could conspire; and change this sorry scheme of things entire; would we not shatter it to bits and mould it closer to our heart's desire.'

Manju put her head on Chandan's shoulders and said, 'I have seen enough of this world. I want no more of it. It will be enough for me if I die in your arms.'

In every hospital comes a time when visitors must depart, and the matron at the nursing home indicated to Khursheed that it was time they all left. Khursheed says she wanted to stay by her sister but the sister would have none of it. 'I'll be

all right here,' my heroine said, 'you go home and look after
the children. I'll see you tomorrow.'

29 March. Early morning, Khursheed arrived at the Home,
tiffin box in hand. 'Your sister has been asking after you,' the
nurse informed Khursheed as she entered Room 26.

'Have you had something to eat?' Meena asked her sister
as she came into the room. Khursheed replied that she had
brought her tiffin from home. 'Then eat it now.' Khursheed
agreed and my heroine joined in with a glass of orange juice.
She seemed in remarkably good spirits.

Madhu had also arrived by now and Meena promised, 'I'll be
home in four days. Then we can all sit together and play cards.'
It looked to the two sisters that their sister would pull through.

It is curious but people always seem to recover just before
death. I am sure there is no medical explanation for this but
I seem to remember so many people who had an almost fatal
lapse, convalesced and had a lapse again.

On 29 March my heroine had a relapse. The pain in the
body increased and by evening she was writhing in agony.
'Please do something,' she told Khursheed, but what could she
do except telephone Dr Shah. He prescribed some tablets.

This night was hell for my heroine. Unable to sleep and
suffering, sometimes crying out in pain, she summoned the
duty nurse many times for help. The nurse could only give
her another tablet.

30 March. A total of eight doctors, each a specialist in
his field, were pressed into service. Each conducted his own
diagnosis and then they all departed for a joint conference.

10 a.m. The eight doctors sent for Khursheed and Amrohi.
Both were impatient for the medical bulletin. Dr Shah was the
spokesman. 'We are sparing no effort but if you wish an honest

answer, we must tell you there is little hope. Even if Meenaji survives this attack she will not live for more than six months.' Prayer he suggested as his ultimate medicine.

Amrohi and Khursheed urged the assembled healers that despite the slender odds the treatment must continue without any slack and every conceivable therapy was to be tried.

Medically, the problem was my heroine's system which was not responding to any of the prescribed drugs, and everything injected in her was being rejected.

As a last resort one of the doctors suggested getting in touch with the surgeon who had treated Meena in London. A foreign mind could possibly help in this crisis.

The trunk call was made and the doctor reached. She remembered the patient of 1968. 'You mean she is still alive?' she asked. She was informed that she was, but just. Was there any new remedy she could suggest? The British doctor answered, not really, but if they wished they could use a recent drug. Even with this antibiotic, she warned, there was remote hope, but as a final resort they could try it.

As death would have it, this particular injection was available only in Europe. Mr O.P. Ralhan, who had come to see my heroine, heard of this problem and promptly rang up a friend in London. He was told by Ralhan to purchase the drug and catch the first available flight to Bombay (the friend arrived eight hours too late). Thus two continents were deployed in saving the great tragedienne.

Typically, when Khursheed went back to her sister's room she did not enquire of the doctor's verdict but whether Khursheed had taken lunch. 'I'll eat only if you have a glass of juice.'

'It's no use. If I drink I'll only bring it up.'

However, the elder sister insisted and both took their

respective meals—the only difference was that Khursheed digested while my heroine vomited immediately.

10.30 a.m. Meena slept and the doctors began intravenous feeding. Near her foot a needle was inserted and the glucose started feeding in. 'What is this?' asked Meena, noticing the ugly apparatus. Khursheed said it was nothing. My heroine went back to sleep again. News, by now, of Meena's indisposition had spread far and wide and colleagues, admirers, exploiters, foes, friends, all started pouring in.

The second-floor telephone was buzzing incessantly. Clearly a telephonist was required to attend to it. Khursheed suggested to family friend Begam Para that they take turns on the telephone outside. 'Since Meena is sleeping now,' Khursheed said, 'I'll take the first watch.'

Around midday Khursheed was busy answering the calls. She had no news for those eager for information. 'Let us pray,' she would invariably reply and keep the receiver back.

Suddenly, Khursheed heard a piercing scream from Room 26. She rushed in. My heroine was sitting up, arms open wide. She was beckoning to her sister. 'Appa, Appa,' she screamed again, *Mein Marna Nahi Chahti*' (I don't want to die).

Hardly had Khursheed gathered my heroine in her arms than she jerked her head to one side and went—went into a coma.

Dr Shah rushed in too. He examined his patient's pulse: it was weak. He examined his patient's blood pressure: it was low. The doctor looked at Khursheed and shook his head. 'Keep trying,' said Khursheed. 'Keep trying.'

Nobody went home that night and a gathering stream of visitors kept coming and going. Saira Banu called and brought with her a flask of tea. The entire Amrohi family was there with the father sitting by Manju's bedside running his hands through her hair.

By 2.30 at night dinner arrived from Rembrandt, and Kamal and his sons had some food and tea in the lobby outside. Immediately after dinner Mr Amrohi came back and took his position near the patient's bed.

Whenever Khursheed went out of the room the nurses looked down and said, 'We are very sorry for your sister.' It was just a matter of time now.

None slept that night except my heroine. She was in a coma.

31 March. A strange whiteness appeared on Meena's body and face. Khursheed, quick to spot this, rang up Dr Shah. He arrived promptly.

The scene in Room 26 is worth recapturing. My heroine was stretched out flat in bed with one oxygen tube in her nose, and another needle inserted through her foot for the glucose. There were not many chairs, so most people in the room were standing. Kamal Amrohi, sitting on the solitary armchair, was crying like a child. An editor of an Urdu magazine and mutual friend of the Amrohis happened to be in the room. 'Manju is going. Please stop her,' he told this friend in a voice bathed with tears.

11 a.m. Dr Shah inserted a third needle in my heroine's body, near the oxygen tube, with the intention of drawing out some liquid. Together the tubes and needles were an ugly sight. Meena's fair body was being pierced. The liquid ejected with the aid of the third needle was colourless.

11.30 a.m. Begam Para could take this hideous sight no more. She approached Dr Shah. Was there any hope? The doctor regretted. 'It won't be long now,' he said, 'if you instruct I will stop the treatment.'

Kamal was consulted. Wouldn't it be a good idea if we stopped torturing Meena's body? Shouldn't her last hours be spent without pain? Chandan agreed but suggested that Manju's sisters be consulted before anything final was done.

The sister (Madhu), praying fervently and still hoping for a miracle, did not agree. The needles continued.

1.30 p.m. The fluid being ejected through the third needle was no longer colourless—it was red, blood red in colour.

Room 26 was capacity-packed and there was a line outside too. (How reminiscent of the cinema halls showing my heroine's films!) Khursheed, Madhu, Shama, Kishore Sharma, Kamal Amrohi and sons were all present. Saira Banu, Nadira, Begum Para, Kammo, Gulzar, Mrs Raiwal, N.S. Kabir were other watchers—these were the only celebrities.

2.30 p.m. My heroine slept sound. But those around her knew; now it was not a question of hours but of minutes. 'For God's sake someone go and get some *Abe Zam Zam* (Holy water from Mecca),' said Begum Para. *Abe Zam Zam* was available but at Landmark. Khursheed's husband Altaf volunteered to dash down to Bandra. He was reminded by a practical soul that Bandra was 16 miles away, and with traffic being what it was his chances of returning on time were slim.

Not deterred, Altaf made preparations to depart, but he was stopped by an actress called Kammo. She said that in her house, which was round the corner, she had some holy water and she would fetch it in a few minutes.

Kammo departed and true to her word returned in time. With the help of a spoon, Khursheed began trickling the blessed water down my heroine's throat. Though technically alive the last rites were being performed.

3.15 p.m. A packed Room 26 was collectively praying. India's No. 1 tragedienne was going fast. A premonition of death filled the room.

3.20 p.m. Khursheed and Madhu were at my heroine's side

looking down at her face, hoping for her eyes to open, praying for the coma to pass away.

3.24 p.m. Meena stirred. 'Munna,' shouted Khursheed. 'Manju,' cried Chandan from near the window where he was standing. But my heroine did not respond. She opened her eyes for a second, surveyed the crowded room, and, eyes open, in the arms of Madhu took her last breath.

3.25 p.m. India's No. 1 tragedienne was dead.

In Room 26 there was crying, shouting, sobbing and wailing. Khursheed had lost her sister, Amrohi had lost his Manju, Gulzar had lost someone he shared artistic moments with, producer Kabir had lost a great actress. To each his own loss. 'When I die,' she had wished many years earlier, 'I would like the following epitaph on my grave:

She ended life with a broken fiddle,
With a broken song,
With a broken heart,
But not a single regret.'

Controversial in life, my heroine was even more controversial in death. Her dead body, to coin a cruel term, was a bone of contention.

Where were they going to bury her? The doctor informed that Meenaji's body was in a state of quick decay. There was a danger that her stomach might erupt. He suggested whatever rites were left undone should be performed in the hospital and the body taken directly from the hospital to the cemetery.[1]

---

1 Whether the doctor said this or not is a matter of hot dispute.

Yes, but which cemetery?

Khursheed said then that Meena had commanded that her body be brought to Landmark, be placed on her bed, and from there it be taken and placed next to Babujee and Majee in the Sunni Kabristan in Bandra.

Mr Amrohi said that Manju had expressed the desire to be buried in Amroha, his native village. He said he had tape-recorded evidence to this effect. (In a Forhans toothpaste–sponsored programme in 1964 my heroine had confessed that she wished to be buried in Amroha, next to her Chandan's grandfather—a venerable holy man.)

Mr A.M. Tariq intervened in the argument. He decided that whatever the evidence, Meena's body must go to Landmark. Kamal agreed and at 5.45 p.m. my heroine, held on the shoulders by her husband and his two sons, was brought down from the second floor of St Elizabeth's Nursing Home and placed inside a waiting ambulance. Tariq was firmly in command of directions and arrangements.

Earlier there had been more confusion. Although a charitable hospital, St Elizabeth's was not letting go a dead body without clearance of the bill. Dr Shah who had received Rs 5,000 from my heroine kept this sum in his own pocket as his previously unpaid fees. So who was going to pay the Home?

Such is the wealth of fact and counter-fact that I am sure I could write a separate book on the payment of this bill. The press, however, was quite definite and their view was echoed in the weekly *Blitz*. They were all in a hurry to bury her, especially Kamal Amrohi, the man who benefited the most during her career. But the shame of it all, nobody came forward to pay the bill of Rs 3,500 at the Nursing Home. The body would have been detained for settlement of the bill but for the kindness of

her personal physician. He sent an S.O.S. to his wife to raise
the amount quickly and the amount was paid.' Subsequently
this press version received wide currency and Amrohi was
branded as the automatic culprit.

Such hydra-headed deceptions have been built around
my heroine's life that it is never easy to establish the truth.
Nevertheless, my own view is that Amrohi is not a mean and
avaricious man. He told me that he offered Dr Shah the money,
but Shah declined saying that since Meena was his patient the
requisition would be made out in his name. He would pay the
hospital then and subsequently forward another bill to Amrohi
for payment (I believe this is customary practice when a patient
is admitted in a hospital through a doctor). For two weeks just
after Meena's death, Mr Amrohi was out of Bombay and in the
ensuing period all the rumours started.

Finally, as soon as Amrohi returned, he sent Shah the
money.

Nobody, including Dr Shah, emerges from this squalid
episode cleanly, but to push all the onus on Amrohi is perhaps
unfair.

The amount of Rs 3,500 agreed, the body was released and
the ambulance made its way back to Landmark, taking precisely
the opposite direction to what it had four days earlier.

Death news travels fast, and when around seven the
ambulance reached Carter Road, there was a crowd of people,
1,000 strong, waiting. The police were summoned to ensure
law and order.

Step by step my heroine was carried to the eleventh floor
and there, through the door marked 'M.K.', she went into
her room, on to her bed—the same bed on which she had
consumed so many lonely hours.

As she lay on her bed there was a curious calm about her. The eyes were closed in a profound and undisturbable sleep. The countenance, though lifeless, wore a serene glow. The lips were parted ever so slightly in a sardonic smile. God, she looked beautiful as a corpse too!

They continued to cry around her, to curse their fate, to pray for resurrection. O! if Meena would only come back—clever woman, she wasn't listening.

Not only was my heroine's room full, but so was the entire house, and so was the landing outside and so was the long line of stairs from the eleventh to the ground floor. To offer condolences the entire film industry presented itself. Jairaj, Bharat Bhushan, Karan Dewan, Raaj Kumar, Shashi Kapoor, Rajendra Kumar, Sanjeev Kumar, Amitabh Bachchan, Anil Dhawan, Navin Nischal, Vinod Mehra, Sujit Kumar, Randhir Kapoor, Sameer, Vinod Khanna, Shatrughan Sinha, Nasir Khan, Iftikhar, Kanhaiya Lal, Sunder and Nana Palsikar.

Among the ladies, Nirupa Roy, Kamini Kaushal, Nimmi, Waheeda Rehman, Sadhna, Nanda, Rakhee, Leena Chandravarkar, Jaya Bhaduri, Radha Saluja, Zahida, Achla Sachdev, Farida Jalal, Seema, Helen, Saeeda Khan, Sardar Akhtar, Naseem Banu and Sitara Devi.

From the producers/directors B.R. Chopra, H.S. Rawail, Kidar Sharma, Devendra Goel, Shakti Samanta, Ramanand Sagar, O.P. Ralhan, Promod Chakravarti, Hrishikesh Mukherjee, N.N. Sippy, K.A. Abbas, Naresh Saigal, Yash Chopra, Premji, Vijay Anand, S.K. Tak, N.S. Kabir, S.M. Sagar; from the musicians, Naushad, Rafi, Talat, S.N. Tripathi, Khayyam, Usha Khanna; from the lyricists, Majrooh, Rajendra Krishna, Hasrat Jaipuri. Also present was Gulshan Nanda who does not fit into any group.

Inside, the Meena Kumari body was being prepared. The 'Gosl' (bath) was ready. Her old clothes were removed, and she was washed and cleaned, powdered and scented. Then the kafan she had purchased especially from Mecca was wrapped round her person. Flowers and garlands were thrown, photographers were told to remain out. The body was ready.

Two schools of thought existed then. Khursheed desired Meena to be buried at Bandra. Mr Amrohi desired to take Manju to his native place for burial. Since Manju was his legally wedded wife he claimed the right to decide cremation. Later he relented on the Amroha trip and agreed on a closer destination—the Shia cemetery at Mazagaon.

My heroine was far away, and for 'Deedar' (last audience) her body was lifted from the bedroom and brought to the main room. According to ritual the first deedar was reserved for Mr Amrohi and he took it. After him a long line of men and women, head bowed, gave their last respects.

At 8 p.m., to the chanting of 'La ilaha illAllah, Muhammad-ur-rasulAllah' (Allah is one and Muhammad is his messenger), the stretcher carrying the body was lifted, and some perceptive neighbour in one of the adjoining flats tuned on the appropriate song *'Inhi Logon Ne Le Leena Dupatta Mera'*. O.P. Ralhan, Rajendra Kumar, Altaf and Kamal Amrohi were the pall-bearers, and as soon as they arrived on the ground floor, they saw Mr Dilip Kumar drive in. Lachrymose, he too lent his shoulder. Now the crowd outside was 3,000 strong and it was unmanageable. Each individual wished to have his own deedar. The police generously used their armaments but to no effect. Meanwhile, the body was trying to reach BMR 8476—the ambulance privileged to carry Meena Kumari on her final travels.

The cortege composed of one ambulance and a dozen cars

moved. Inside BMR 8476 sat Kamal Amrohi and his two sons, Dilip Kumar, O.P. Ralhan and Rajendra Kumar.

From Bandra to Mahim to Dadar to Byculla and then to Dr Mascarenhas Road and then to 'Rehmata Baug'. A call had been made and a grave dug north to south (never east to west among Muslims) and kept ready. Naturally, such an eminent death cannot be kept a secret and around Mascarenhas Road word was passing that the body of Meena Kumari would soon be coming that way.

I went to Rehmata Baug too—much later—and saw my heroine's grave. It was pathetic. I couldn't believe that the woman they called India's greatest tragedienne would finally end up like this. This Shia cemetery must be the most unkempt of Shia cemeteries in India. Grass grows wild, the ground is uneven and stony, and all around there is poverty and desolation. The day I went to Rehmata Baug some fresh flowers had been scattered on the grave courtesy a fan from Bahrein. Just before me two schoolgirls had come and stood in silence. 'Kamal Amrohi, who owes everything to Meena Kumari, never comes. Khursheed comes sometime,' said the priest looking after this show. 'This is the way the world is,' he concluded philosophically and sadly.

10 p.m. The funeral procession arrived at the cemetery and trouble was in store. A group of nearly 6,000 fans was jostling and pushing. The ambulance was having to move very slowly. Patrolling policemen vainly tried to hold the crowd back. Someone suggested Mr Dilip Kumar use his magnetic personality in controlling the crowd.

With some difficulty the ambulance reached inside the cemetery, and there, inside the modest mosque, namaz was said. Mr Dharmendra, who had joined the farewell, too donned a white handkerchief and raised his hands to the sky. 'Forgive the deceased her sins and grant her eternal peace O Allah,' was the substance of the prayer.

10.30 p.m. The procession moved towards the pit. Kamal Amrohi's two sons jumped inside and very gently my heroine's body, wrapped in the blessed 'kafan' and a white shawl, covered with flowers, was carefully laid on earth. Then her face, which was covered, was opened, and turned towards the holy city. Chandan crying his heart out got lost in the crowd.

'Kamal Sahab,' shouted a voice. He was required to conclude the funeral. 'Ya Allah!' said Kamal, finding his way, and picked up a handful of mud. He threw it into the pit. And then everybody joined. Mighty film stars, relatives, Urdu writers and the thousands of unknowns.

10.45 p.m. India's No. 1 tragedienne was dead and buried.

JAGDISH AURANGABADKAR

Answering her fan mail

A sumptuous dinner:
Meena Kumari had a
weakness for basi roti

A game of rummy with Kamal Amrohi

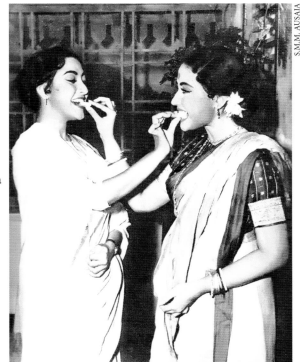

With Mala Sinha

Meena Kumari's sister Madhu with her husband Mehmood

Hindustan Lever signed Meena Kumari
as its brand ambassador for Lux soap in 1953,
barely a year after she debuted as a heroine in *Baiju Bawra*

With Dharmendra, the love of her life

The Many

Faces of

Meena Kumari

In *Bachchon Ka Khel* (1946)

In *Baiju Bawra* (1952), a star is born: the reviews of the film were ecstatic and as one magazine put it, 'the promising new star [Meena] will be ranked among the first five stars of the year on the merit of her outstanding acting in *Baiju Bawra*'

In *Aladdin and the Lamp* (1952), her last film with Homi Wadia who cast her in a number of mythologicals

With Dilip Kumar in *Azad* (1955), a 'tarted-up version of the Robin Hood fable', one of her rare forays into light-hearted roles

In *Dil Apna Aur Preet Parayi* (1960), where Meena Kumari 'played the nurse sacrificing everything for the glory of Florence Nightingale'

Publicity poster for *Chandni Chowk* (1954), director B.R. Chopra's maiden effort: 'In a difficult role,' wrote *Filmfare*, 'Meena Kumari turns in a superb portrayal … an outstanding example of her histrionic talent'

Meena Kumari starred opposite Pradeep Kumar in quite a few films, including Kidar Sharma's *Chitralekha* (1964) and *Aarti* (1962): she received a *Filmfare* nomination for Best Actress for *Aarti* (below), in a year when all three nominations for the Best Actress Award went to her (the others being for *Sahib Bibi Aur Ghulam* and *Main Chup Rahungi*)

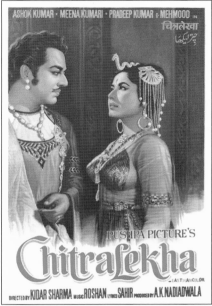

ASHOK KUMAR · MEENA KUMARI · PRADEEP KUMAR & MEHMOOD IN

चित्रलेखा

PUSHPA PICTURE'S

Chitralekha

EASTMANCOLOR

DIRECTED BY KIDAR SHARMA MUSIC ROSHAN LYRICS SAHIR PRODUCED BY A.K. NADIADWALA

On the sets of Bimal Roy's *Do Bigha Zameen* (1953)
in which she had a small role

अशोक कुमार · मीना कुमारी
आशित बरन

शरद्चंद्र कृत

परिणीता

PARINEETA
दिग्दर्शक बिमल रॉय संगीत अरूणकुमार

Publicity poster for
Bimal Roy's *Parineeta*
(1953): 'As Lalita …
she was at once candid,
calculating and sweet …
and demonstrated that
she was an actress of
considerable and perhaps
untapped talent'

Publicity poster for
Satta Bazaar (1959)

Publicity poster for *Phool Aur
Patthar* (1966): its success
established the Dharam–Meena
team as a winner

In *Pakeezah* (1972), her swansong, and one of her
most celebrated performances

KAMAT FOTO FLASH

As Chhoti Bahu in *Sahib Bibi Aur Ghulam* (1962), her greatest performance: 'the mental picture of Meena Kumari which comes readily to mind is from Guru Dutt's *Sahib Bibi Aur Ghulam*'

NATIONAL FILM ARCHIVE OF INDIA

Publicity poster for *Pakeezah* (1972)

In *Pakeezah* (1972): no one played grief-stricken roles with as much aplomb as Meena Kumari. 'In movies like *Parineeta, Dil Apna Aur Preet Parayi, Pakeezah*, she either dies or is abandoned by her man'

Section Two
Personal Appraisal

SEVEN

How I Got to Know Her

There is nothing much deader than a dead motion picture actor.

— John Dos Passos

'We would like you to write a book on Meena Kumari. Are you interested?' the voice asked over the telephone.

'Yes,' I replied.

'Good. I will come over and see you tomorrow to finalize the arrangements,' concluded the voice as it kept the receiver back on the hook.

I relate this telephonic conversation in its entirety simply to point out how casually and with what brazenness I accepted my publisher's commission. You would imagine that I was a veteran writer of biographies? No. You would imagine that I was intimately acquainted with the subject (Meena Kumari)? No. You would imagine that I had access (at that time) to some vital and breathtaking inside information? No. You would imagine that I was a fool? No, not entirely.

So why did I accept the enormous task of compiling a

complete and comprehensive biography of Meena Kumari, with the recklessness that I did? Basically, two reasons. One, I had just published a faintly successful book which, even if it didn't quite outsell the Segals and the Harold Robbins, was doing quite nicely and had established me as a writer of some merit, possibly dubious merit. Now this kind of quick gain can be heady and sometimes dangerous. Like the first-time gambler who, after having had his share of luck, feels he can sweep the jackpot, the writer with beginner's luck too feels that nothing is beyond his pen: avant-garde fiction, lullabies, film scripts, biographies—you name it, he can write it. These were, I must acknowledge, the sort of delusions I was suffering from, and I offer them in the hope that they justify or at least partially explain my unwarranted confidence—substantiating my long-held belief that delusions can sometimes be useful.

The other reason was that the woman whose portrait I had been asked to sketch interested me immensely—not while she was alive, but once she was dead. I suppose this sounds callous, but it is true. In the timing and manner of her death my heroine assumed heroic dimensions, crystallized the essential human travesty involved in being what is cheaply known as a 'star', and brought to surface a many-sided and complex personality which had been current all the time, but alas undiscovered.

As an individual I knew nothing about her beyond the tittle-tattle I had read in showbiz mags or heard from unreliable friends given to dropping names. (I once heard a chap expound at great length the gory details of my heroine's affair with Dharmendra. He concluded every sentence with, 'Arre Bhai Dharmendra told me this himself'.) The source of my interest in Meena Kumari, I must point out, was not direct; rather it was nourished through another woman (white, naturally) who in my juvenile fantasy years exercised an erotic and emotional influence which I will not even begin to analyse. The woman was Marilyn Monroe and though my heroine and this woman performed thousands of miles apart there were several parallels. Publicly they had little in common; behind the scenes they were sisters. The same legendary physical powers, the same unfulfilled relationships, the same consuming irresistible wistfulness, the same self-destructive urges.

(You can't imagine my joy when I subsequently learnt that one of my heroine's favourite stars was Marilyn Monroe, and on many occasions she was known to have discussed the sad fate of this woman. Even on her deathbed in the nursing home Meena Kumari spoke to Gulzar about Marilyn Monroe.)

Once I had signed on the dotted line and promised to deliver so many thousand words, I began examining seriously my own credentials for writing this book. And the more I examined, the more apparent it became that, on the surface, I was uniquely unqualified for such an undertaking. To begin with I had never met my subject in the flesh. This in particular depressed me because every hack in Bombay masquerading as journalist, writer, director and producer had spent some time with her. I used to get so unmanageable when I used to read that Mr So-and-so had a long conversation with my heroine in her flat at Carter Road, Bandra. There was no end, it appeared, to these people who called on her, made demands on her courtesy, while she listened to them with rare and exemplary politeness, and made them cups of tea ('*Tum Kya Karoge Sunkar Mujhse Meri Kahani*'—What good will it do listening to my story—she told one of them). The only person who did not set eyes on her was me.

There is, I know, no huge reason to get worked up about

this. Contact and conversation with subject is not essential to biography (some of the finest life stories have been written hundreds of years after the death of the person concerned. Henri Troyat's *Life of Tolstoy*, universally acknowledged as one of the best biographies written, is a recent book). But I remain at heart a passionate believer in personal chemistry. The reaction and equation that take place when two people meet is for me worth a thousand words. Of course I could talk to people, rustle up the archives, see her old films, contact her sisters, but she still didn't make me a cup of tea. And God knows if she had what would have transpired, what illuminating insights I would have brought back for you.

You think these were my only doubts when I began writing this book!

I left India in 1962 and returned in 1969. As a result I was completely cut off from the Bombay cinema, and more importantly from Meena Kumari (incidentally, the last film I saw before I boarded my plane was *Sahib Bibi Aur Ghulam*). There was thus a glaring gap in my knowledge of the star's activities. Before I left she was still our leading lady; when I returned she had descended to playing the fallen woman, the elder sister, the widowed wife of Indian cinema. What happened in the intervening years?

My most pressing problem, however, was one of attitude. Like every third person in Bombay I had views on cinema and some pretty radical remedies on how to civilize the one in India (I had outlined some of these notions in my last book). If the Bombay cinema then left me cold, not so the Bombay film world. I had met some of our stars, studied the workings of the industry, seen a few films being shot, and I had quietly decided that I wanted nothing to do with these people. I envied them their opportunities and it made me sick to see how they squandered them. For sheer vulgarity, dandyism, shallowness, squalor and dishonesty the Bombay film world is hard to beat. Any industry which can pay nine lakhs of rupees for one contract to one star should be publicly prosecuted and banned. This is the way I felt and I wondered how I could write an unbiased account of a woman totally and irredeemably immersed in this world. Was there not a danger that my prejudices would seep through? Could I keep my head about me?

Who then, I speculated, were the people most qualified to write an authoritative biography on my heroine? Mr Amrohi? Certainly. He had known her from the tender age of six, married her at twenty, and lived with her twelve long years. If anybody had the key to the Meena Kumari crossword, surely he must. I could see them sitting together late in the night, lights dimmed, glasses filled,[1] talking of love, poetry, death, music ... what a treasure house of fascinating memories he must have! My only consolation is that Mr Amrohi is not a writer of biographies and is usually too busy making his films. Though, if he ever attempted a book on his wife, and wrote it with honesty and wit, it would be superb. Will he?

Gulzar is different. And he worries me. He worries me because I have more respect for him as a writer than I have for Mr Amrohi. Not only did he know my heroine closely for a period of years, but he is also a cunning, urbane and sane man. (A fear which was confirmed after my first visit to his flat at Pali Hill. When I told him I was writing a biography of

---

1 Mr Amrohi rarely drinks so we can assume that the glasses were full of tea.

Meena Kumari, he put one hand on my knee and said skilfully, 'Well we are both engaged in an honourable task.') To my mind Gulzar is the only authentic screenwriter this country has produced, the only one who has understood the medium and disciplined his art to suit it. To compound my gloom I now learn that my heroine bequeathed her diaries to him. One can be sure that Mr Gulzar will make good use of them. (I read somewhere that he intends publishing a complete biography of Meena Kumari next year. I avidly look forward to it.)

In all probability there are lots of others: chamchas, nannies, servants, flatterers, secretaries, who could write a few hundred pages, but I am not bothered by them. They would only write a book on my heroine if there was money in it.

What hope then for me? Is there any reason why my version of Meena Kumari should have any mileage?

Yes, there is. When the Amrohis and Gulzars sit down to write they may come face-to-face with impeding obstacles; obstacles erected by propriety, vested interests and skeletons in the cupboard. They may discover that familiarity in biography can breed contempt. There are dangers of being overtly sentimental with perhaps too much emphasis on personal grief. And the biggest danger of all: how do you suddenly become detached and objective about a person you have known for ten years or lived with? Was a cool and calculated assessment possible by these people?

So, finally, I decided that my not knowing my subject could possibly be an advantage; that there may be some virtue in the outsider looking in, with no axe to grind, no fear of trampling sensitive toes, no personal interest (except to write a good book). An alien unattached view may get closer to the truth about this woman than an inside one.

These, anyway, were the arguments I was trying to marshal and deploy in my favour. I would be the first to accept that I did not have a mighty arsenal. My weaknesses were manifold but so were my strengths. Whatever I lacked in terms of inside information, background knowledge, etc., I was determined to make up by industry and research.

With unnatural enthusiasm and zest did I set about reviving my heroine's past life. The meaning of the cliché hard work was making sense to me. Finally every scrap of information, every press release, every review, every third-rate line of gossip, every sentence uttered, lay securely in my possession. Deep into the years I went. Dusty 1952 *Filmfares*, difficult to attain 1958 *Screens*, impossible 1953 *Film-Indias*. I sat patiently going through them all making copious notes. A mountainous and bewildering library was in my possession which allowed me to reconstruct the history of my heroine with some precision.

Then began the interviews—and here again I spared no effort. Anybody, absolutely anybody, who had spent five seconds with my heroine was of use to me. And I remember with some bitterness how some of the big boys kept me waiting: 'No. Mr Dharmendra cannot see you tomorrow. He has nothing to say on the subject. Ring back next month.'

Once, I spent nearly thirty rupees trying to reach Pali Hill where my heroine's secretary was living. He welcomed me in encouragingly but when I told him the reason for my visit, he said politely but crisply, 'Sorry, can't tell you anything.' I shook his hand and left.

I also discovered that the people closest to my heroine were precisely the people who told me nothing. Yes, they would give me cups of tea (a standard ritual, I believe), smile indulgently, make some asinine remark about my long hair (one of them called me a Hippie) and pronounce, 'She was a great actress, Mehta Sahab.' However, when I asked a straight or honest question they promptly buttoned up. 'What sort of book are you going to write?' one of them asked sarcastically.

Mercifully, this chase had its lighter moments. I called on the house of a now forgotten actor who had starred opposite my heroine. He was delighted to see me and obviously flattered that someone had come to solicit his view. He spoke at length, not about my heroine but the acclaim he had received. I tried discreetly to guide him to the subject, but he was adamant and scarcely said a word about my heroine. I emerged from his house two hours later none the wiser about Meena Kumari but packed with information about him.

Were it not for these diversions, I suspect I would have collapsed mentally and physically under the weight of calling and re-calling on the luminaries. All in all a salutary experience and next time someone rings me up and asks me to write a book on a film star, I'll have an answer ready.

Sometime towards the beginning of July an important event occurred. I had returned after one more interview with 'someone who knew'. Five more pages of notes were added to my burgeoning file. However, for some time now I had become increasingly aware that all this accumulated copy was crushing me down, leading me up the wrong track. The bloodhound in me warned that the scent was false. My researches, travels and meetings had been productive as expected. From the archives I got facts, from colleagues I got opinions. Facts piled upon opinions and more facts and more opinions, and in the process something crucial had escaped. I was skimming on the surface with a simulated image of my heroine, an image made up of moth-eaten files and second-hand impressions. I had to get talking to her. I had to see things her way, and no interview, no magazine cutting could help me there. If anything I required black magic.

That evening I decided to change gear. I was sitting in my room depressed and distinctly unhappy with the way the biography was going. Almost all writers during the course of a manuscript get to a stage when they have the feeling that things are going wrong, that they have screwed up a great opportunity—what Hemingway used to call 'the bad days'. I opened a bottle of rum (my heroine would undoubtedly appreciate the gesture) and my Meena Kumari scrap book. I started thumbing through her pictures. Halfway through, I stopped as if struck by lightning. In front of me was a photo of my heroine, not a still borrowed from a film, but an off-the-scenes picture. I kept staring at it for God knows how many minutes ... and suddenly I saw light. There, staring me in the face were all the answers I was looking for. On that impossibly beautiful and alternately, achingly human face, was mirrored, crystal clear, the story of my heroine's life. My spirits were lifted.

There was a bonus for me when I played her long-playing record. 'I write, I recite.' All those forlorn poems on the inevitability of death and the crushing loneliness of life, put to music by Khayyam, had their own story to tell. I am not being melodramatic, but that one picture of my heroine and that one record were worth all the 'informed views' I had gathered in two months.

The routine subsequently became pleasurable. Late at night I would gaze at her picture while the record player sung her ghazals. And as each night vanished I felt I had come a little closer in my understanding of this woman.

Today, a month later, sitting at my writing table, the question I would like to pose to my heroine, wherever she may be, is this: 'Meenaji, no one can ever hope to completely dissect and analyse another human being. I have done as much as is humanly possible as far as collecting fact and opinion is concerned. But you know that there is little truth in what other people say. I am not an ambitious man. If in these 200-odd pages I have been able to compress three Meena Kumari truths, which you yourself would confirm, I shall think I have succeeded.'

EIGHT

The Actress

I think you have to be schizoid three different ways to be an actor. You've got to be three different people. You have to be a human being. Then you have to be the character you are playing. And on top of that you've got to be the guy sitting in Row 10, watching yourself and judging yourself. That's why most of us are crazy to start with or go nuts once we get into it. I mean, don't you think it's a pretty spooky way to earn a living?

– George C. Scott

Overpraise, someone once said, in the end is the most damaging kind of praise.

Shortly after her suicide in 1963, Marilyn Monroe's reputation rocketed sky-high. Overnight, critics became dogged devotees and a whole host of film and non-film people suddenly discovered that Miss Monroe was possibly the finest actress, apart from being the sex symbol of the post-war Hollywood years. Even the more resolute of her belittlers went about mouthing the most tendentious high-falutin rubbish about her talent. All a case of being charitable to the dead, I suppose.

Something similar is beginning to happen to my heroine. In the latter period of her life, and particularly since her death, the sweet, syrupy, unreliable sound of undiluted acclaim can be heard everywhere. Sentiment has overtaken scrutiny and the epitaph is as universal as it is simple and definitive. 'Meena Kumari was an incomparable, superb artiste the like of whom will not be seen for many decades to come.' Epitaph concluded. No further argument.

Now, as a rule, I am sceptical of the Bombay film world and my instinct is to disbelieve most of its judgements. Knowing my heroine a little I think she too would be annoyed and irritated by this blanket of undebated praise; annoyed not because she wasn't worthy of it, but because no one has bothered to build up a cogent case for it.

Hoping to correct this error in this personal appraisal I am going to proceed along slightly different lines. I am at once going to cross-examine and deliver a verdict; I am going to ask questions and then answer them—all in an effort to put my heroine in her rightful place.

Was she really a great actress? If so how did this greatness manifest itself on the screen? Was she truly versatile or was her genius restricted to a pattern of performance? Was there any particular acting period in which this greatness was most pronounced? Was she a uniformly great actress or was she erratic and fitfully great?

This might be about the right time to inject a note of heresy in this discussion. Is it possible that Meena Kumari was not a great actress? Is it possible that she valiantly attempted to assail the peak of greatness and slipped? Is it possible that she was just a competent or fairly competent actress? You may think that such questions are blasphemous or irreverent; but not my heroine. Such is her confidence, I suspect, that she would willingly grant permission to interrogate from all angles.

Consequently, we are going to put Meena Kumari's career on the operating table, and for surgical instruments we are going to use thirty-six long and full years of her screen life. Fortunately, abundant material exists for this operation (seventy-seven films) and its success will depend solely on one factor: that this operation be conducted by cold, clinical, impartial yet sympathetic hands—hands which are not contaminated by either subservience or sycophancy.

But before we begin this operation we must define, or at least attempt to define, what great acting is. For I have an uneasy feeling that some of us overuse this word 'great' and perhaps by overuse we have undervalued it. What do we mean when we say Dilip Kumar was great in *Devdas* or Rajesh Khanna in *Anand* or Jane Fonda in *Klute*? Probably we are unsure of the exact meaning and implications of great acting, and nothing better than a good solid word like great to cover up this confusion.

A word of warning here is essential. Definitions by definition are faulty. No two sentences can ever hope to embrace and compress the myriad facets of great acting. What they can do, however, is lay down a framework, enunciate some ground rules for us to measure Meena Kumari's prowess. So define we must.

Khwaja Ahmed Abbas, possibly our most devoted and commercially luckless directors, has, I think, an oversimplified, nevertheless noteworthy, interpretation. 'Great acting,' he says, 'is when you feel that the person is not acting.' For Abbas a completely unselfconscious rendering of the part is the essence.

George C. (*Patton*) Scott, who has never had formal acting lessons in his life, is nearer the mark when he says, 'The only measurement of fine acting is so simple, yet so many actors get fouled up about it. It's this: Does the audience feel it? It doesn't matter a damn what the actor does or feels—it's what the lady with the blue hat down there is feeling. You as an actor can suffer agonies, but unless that is communicated to the people, you've failed.' Satyajit Ray on the other hand thinks that a great performer is someone 'who continues to be expressive or interesting even after he or she has stopped doing anything ... and it includes anyone who keeps his calm before the camera, projects a personality and evokes sympathy.'

The definition I endorse comes from the eminent English critic C.E. Montague. For him great acting is simply the sum of three strict elements: 1) A plastic physical medium, 2) A finished technical cunning, 3) A passion of joy in the thought of the character acted. The reason I endorse this last definition is because it breaks up Great Acting into its individual salient ingredients, and if these ingredients are present in a performance, one can be reasonably certain that the lady with the blue hat will have received it.

That my heroine was blissfully unfamiliar with these definitions is perfectly proper. In her own words, 'I shall never be able to decide what exactly is the formula for best acting and how it's done, because I am merely an actress and will never be anything more than that.' Like George C. Scott, Meena Kumari believed that the burden of final judgement was not hers but yours and mine.

When Montague talks of a physical medium in his tripartite ideal, he is talking about the body which for a performing artiste, be he a circus tiger or dancer Helen, is a basic. The body, to state the obvious, is made up of separate entities, hands, eyes, legs, nose, mouth, voice, etc. In great acting, the body, collectively, is fused into the performance, thus investing it with added authenticity and credibility. By fusing I mean using the organs, like a potter uses clay, to aid, abet and heighten the dramatic impact of the performance. Anybody who has seen Charlie Chaplin on the screen will know what I mean. That little man cast and conducted his not-too-large or impressive physical medium so that his unforgettable tramp took on added dimensions of reality. The body and Chaplin were inseparable. Similarly, to great acting a plastic physical medium is important; one which is so malleable that it can be changed, channelled and chiselled to suit the requirements of the representation.

I admit that this discipline is extremely difficult to achieve, and one can literally count on one's left hand the number of artistes who possess or possessed it. Laurence Olivier has it, Marlon Brando has it. Charlie Chaplin had it. Not many others.

Among our own stars this attribute is almost non-existent. The reason for this is that the roles expected of them are so physically undemanding that usually there is no need for Montague's first ideal. Additionally, and ignorantly, our stars feel that all visual wants of a part can be met successfully by their make-up man—given a false beard, a bit of wig and a dab of paint nothing is impossible. I saw Sharmila Tagore play an old woman and it was quite laughable at how messed up she got. I saw no perception of age in the acting and despite her painted wrinkles, she gave no intimations of the fifty years she was supposed to represent.

My heroine is vulnerable here too—although she was the only one who gave occasional glimpses of her ability to use her body. Alas, like all the others, she was quickly put into a slot. When she was a girl, they made her play young girl parts; when she became a heroine she got heroine parts; and finally when she became the elder sister she got elder sister parts. I would have loved for example to see her play a blind woman or a lame woman or a prostitute (not the 'nautch girl' genteel variety but the Foras Road stuff) or a wicked sister-in-law. As things stand, in all honesty I cannot conclusively answer whether she truly had an elastic physical medium or not. She certainly had a degree of it, but there isn't enough evidence in the can for an emphatic yes.

The glimpses were there. In *Mere Apne*, as the old woman lured into the big city, she imparts with the aid of her quizzical look and white hair some hint of what it feels to be old and bewildered. Doddering along the street, her posture slightly bent, she looks every inch the woman she is supposed to be. We saw another glimpse in Abbas's *Char Dil Char Rahen* in which she played a cobbler's woman. Wearing a tattered sari, squatting barefoot on the ground, she seemed to achieve almost naturally the rustic and earthy dignity of her people.

These glimpses leave me sanguine that she was endowed with Montague's first attribute. These, and two other things which were outstandingly unique and elastic: her voice and her eyes.

The eyes first. Never before have I seen in an actress's eyes such power, such resentment, such pathos, such chastity, such love, such—to use an Urdu metaphor—intoxication. If I sound a little ecstatic about my heroine's eyes it's because like most men, I am an 'eyes man', and Meena Kumari deployed hers with devastating effect.

They were never remarkable—the eyes, in shape, structure

or size; she used hardly any cosmetics, except a thin line of 'kaajal' extending towards the corners. But those studded gems on her face were capable of intimidating the most seasoned of stars. 'Even Dilip Kumar found it difficult to keep his calm in front of her,' I was told by a director.

In *Phool Aur Patthar* her eyes taunt and heap ridicule on her rapacious relatives when the final confrontation takes place in court, while only a few frames earlier those very eyes were exuding all the stirrings of love recognized and returned. In *Dushman* there is one scene of vivid vindictiveness. The entire village has forgiven convict Rajesh Khanna, and my heroine watches this unforgivingly from her modest hut. Then with one piercing rapier-sharp gaze rebukes the village. She does not utter a syllable, yet her eyes shout thunderingly: 'How can you forgive the man who murdered my husband?'

Consumed with alcohol in *Sahib Bibi Aur Ghulam* she lounges on the bed, sings a song '*Na Jao Sayiyyan*', emits ounces of erotica without removing a single garment, and entreats with her husband to stay back. From vindictiveness to erotica to tenderness is, I suppose, the extreme. Yet in how many films those same eyes have expressed the purest and cleanest emotions of tenderness usually towards an infant or a child? In *Gomti Ke Kinare* a lost child looking for his mother grabs hold of my heroine in a temple. She has never laid eyes on the child before but the way she looks at him, so full of filial and motherly love, that the child is convinced he has found what he came looking for. The examples are innumerable and the conclusion must be that my heroine could perform minor miracles with her eyes, and no one, safe to say, on the Indian screen could match hers—for me even when judged from the mean standard of beauty.

If she was good with the eyes, she was equally good with
the voice. Having been brought up in a Muslim household
and environment, she had built-in advantages when it came
to speaking Hindustani. Always her diction was chaste, clean,
literate and well rounded. She never mumbled—except
when necessary—or ever got her emphasis wrong. To these
inherited qualities she added her own distinctive inventiveness
and range.

Assiduously, through dedicated homework, she cultivated
an extremely sharp and fine ear for sound, and her ability
to reproduce accents and dialects totally alien to her was
uncanny. In Abbas's *Char Dil Char Rahen* she was required to
speak the way they do in Haryana. She asked Abbas to give
her some idea of this accent only once. Then Abbas says, 'She
copied it perfectly. I couldn't believe that she had picked it
up so soon.'

Abrar Alvi highlights the sound perfectionist in her. When
Guru Dutt first makes contact with my heroine in *Sahib Bibi Aur
Ghulam* she is supposed to say 'Aao' pause 'Idher Aao' (come,
come here). Alvi wished her to say this in a specific manner
and she couldn't quite get it. But she kept on trying 'Aao Idher
Aao' until she got it right. There was, Alvi told me, 'no need for
her to keep on because we were quite satisfied with her initial
rendering.' No need for Mr Alvi, but for my heroine nothing
short of the perfect would do.

Even in her earlier films like *Baiju Bawra*, when she was hardly
twenty, the respect for phonetics was there, and the diction
remained feminine, deep, full-throated and never shrill. Too
many of our present-day stars speak from the area of the mouth;
my heroine went down a little and from some mysterious inner
reserve produced the sounds of music.

Control was her single major virtue. In *Phool Aur Patthar*, on the witness stand she proclaims her lover's defence with mounting strength. The end of her appeal is climactic and frenzied. 'This man,' she blares, pointing at Dharmendra, 'is no criminal. He is a god. He is a god. He is a god.' And breaks down. As I watched and heard her enact this scene I thought that in the mouth of any other actress these words would possibly sound preposterous, totalitarian and excessive; in the mouth of my heroine they seemed both normal and reserved.

She could be soft and serene too. In Bimal Roy's *Parineeta*, a predominantly tranquil and quiet movie, she does not put a word wrong. This quietness, when needed, could take on shapes of incipient intimacy. In *Badbaan*, faced with her gone away childhood sweetheart (Dev Anand), she blushes violently as she says, 'I have recognized you. You have not recognized me.' Now if you examine these lines, you will see how unenterprising, unintelligent and ridiculous they are. To acquire some respectability, therefore, you require a rendering which combines bashfulness and playfulness with just a tinge of regret and rebuke. Go and hear my heroine in *Badbaan* accomplish this impossible combination faultlessly.

Melody was always present in her voice and this probably because she was a singer of sorts. No Lata Mangeshkar, Meena Kumari, as her recorded ghazals testify, could hum a decent tune. In fact when she was a child star she had lent her voice for playback singing. I think this sense of melody aided her in appreciating rhythm in speech: the value of the pause, the importance of weight and tone, the need for succinctness when delivering the punch line.

Ambitious and budding entrants into the film line could do

worse than sit down every evening and listen to my heroine's sounds. (Miss Zeenat Aman who speaks Hindi like a character straight out of John Masters should begin right away.)

Almost everyone but me is convinced that Meena Kumari was a woman of stunning beauty. Bewitching woman, exquisite woman, beautiful woman (*Filmfare* in 1952 called her a 'pastoral beauty'), these are the meaningless terms in which she is usually described. My own view is that she was not in any orthodox sense 'pretty'— at least not till 1962.

The early Meena Kumari was a mild-complexioned, 164 cm tall, plain-looking woman. She was the kind of girl you would pass on the street without blinking an eyelid. How plain-looking she was became transparently apparent to me in the film *Badbaan* in which she had Usha Kiron as co-star and competitor. In many of the sequences—especially when they appear together—Usha Kiron is demonstrably more attractive. My heroine with her unaffected homespun naturalness was no match for the gorgeous rosy-cheeked Usha Kiron.

Meena Kumari didn't exactly look like a million dollars: the face was oval, uneventful and flat, the features had no definition or symmetry, the countenance had little arresting brilliance. Actually her plainness was writ large on her face. Yet I think my heroine's looks were her fortune. Had she been burdened by customary prettiness she would have been lumbered with glamorous, mindless roles. Her somewhat nondescript face gave her a mobility which enabled her to move artistically in a moderately wide circle.

Anyway, women with beautiful faces are bores. They use their beauty as some kind of trump card which they feel is capable of seeing them through all situations. My heroine did not have a pretty face; she had something much better—an interesting face, and it became even more interesting when she reached the age of thirty in 1962. This is the age of prime for a woman and my heroine's front appropriately blossomed and flowered. Sensuousness was absent, but in its place present was sobriety and nobility and delicacy.

Her whole bearing had a built-in poise. You never felt there was anything phony or artificial about her. Whatever beauty she owned was intrinsic. What a relief from the leading ladies of today—personally, with them, I can't tell where the Max Factor ends and the real woman begins.

Beauty, incidentally, is a subjective concept. What is beautiful for one person may be ugly for another. For myself, I think, she was a woman of exclusive charm. I find nuances of sadness on a woman's face fatally irresistible, because one always assumes that with sadness there is depth, there is detachment, there is serenity and there is hidden passion. Those dark circles under my heroine's eyes, that look of having seen it all, that ironical half-smile, have you seen these recently on our screen? I think not.

The point, however, must be made that in an industry which values 'looks' above everything else, my heroine's achievements with her fundamental disabilities were all the more meritorious.

All this leads to questions of versatility. No, she was not a versatile actress. I say this with a certain amount of regret because the phrase *Great Tragedienne* is just about sticking in my throat. Every line written about Meena Kumari is preceded by these two words.

Initially, I began wondering whether my heroine was another victim of our producers' mammoth capacity for putting people in pigeonholes for one lifetime at least. Since

her first success, *Baiju Bawra*, was a conventional tragedy role
I thought our cinema moghuls had gleefully pushed Meena
Kumari into this stereotype. I was searching frantically for
some ammunition to explode this tragedienne myth and state
that Meena Kumari could have been a *Great Comedienne* too.
Despite a back-breaking search I have not been able to find
this ammunition and I must go along with the consensus that,
to put it at its worst, crying was my heroine's forte.

She did get two or three opportunities to break away: *Ilzam*
opposite Kishore Kumar, *Kohinoor* opposite Dilip Kumar,
Miss Mary opposite Gemini Ganesan (all described as 'breezy
comedies'). But she wasn't entirely at ease. She made the same
admission herself when she said, 'Only I know how difficult
it was to play these roles.' Why she felt a kinship, attachment
and fondness for tragedy is another matter, and I propose to
elucidate that in the next chapter where I will be examining
not the actress but the person. Sufficient to say here that my
heroine was at her best when portraying the woes of life as
seen by our film-makers.

Versatility, however, is not crucial to a great actress. If her
range is restricted to a sphere, this is undoubtedly limiting, but
the more important consideration is the excellence she brings
to that sphere. And anyway, versatility on the Indian screen
is as common as a dinosaur. I can think of only one performer
who has it in some measure and that is Dilip Kumar, and even
he had to fight furiously to get out of his earlier morose and
morbid straightjacket.

If my heroine was a *Great Tragedienne*, she travelled the gamut.
The variety, surprisingly, that exists in tragedy is infinite (life
essentially being tragic). And Meena Kumari played every
conceivable unhappy part. Drowning midstream hand-in-hand

in *Baiju Bawra*, jumping off a cliff to atone for some sexual sin in *Jawab*, having her husband crushed under a truck in *Dushman*, catching a terrible disease in *Daera*, dancing on broken glass in *Pakeezah* ... Yes there was perpetual pain, but what superiority she brought to it. (Informed cinema people regret that the foremost female tragedienne was never matched with the foremost male tragedienne. Dilip Kumar and Meena did get together in *Footpath* in 1952, but subsequently they were always in films like *Kohinoor*, etc., which demanded no tragic skills. 'Had they matched she would have taught him a thing or two,' I was told.)

Nothing enlightens us about her restricted versatility better than her unceasing quest for challenging and taxing roles. Khwaja Ahmed Abbas told me a lovely story in this context. He had gone to see my heroine with a script in which there were three female roles. Abbas, privately, had decided that she would be best suited to one of these—the one which was the most unglamorous and also the most exacting. However, he decided that he would let my heroine make her own choice. Abbas read out his script during a three-hour session. She listened patiently without disturbing him once. As soon as Abbas finished, she said, 'I want the role of the cobbler's woman.' This was precisely the role Abbas had in mind for her and he told me that his respect for my heroine from that day onwards increased tenfold.

And now technical cunning.

Consider this: a famous star, a famous studio, a famous film. Everything is ready and waiting to do the sad scene. The director shouts 'action', the lights go on, the camera rolls. Just then the famous film star puts up his hand. 'A minute,' he says, 'I forgot to put glycerin in my eyes.' This true and revealing incident illustrates the ragbag of crutches unaccomplished and technically deficient stars (you'd be surprised how many we have) need to see them through their parts. Next time you see a tear-laden face on the screen, don't be fooled. It's all ointment.

My heroine was an exception. She required no glycerin. Tears came to her eyes when she desired them to come, and this is just one instance of the finished technical cunning, that arsenal of small gestures and cinema skill, Meena Kumari possessed.

In a way it's understandable. From nearly the day she opened her eyes my heroine found herself in front of the camera, and in twenty-odd years she imbibed all the intricacies and minutiae of cinema-acting craft: at what angle to face the lens, how best to make an entry into a scene, the choice of mannerism, cultivating a special idiosyncrasy, using the correct artifact for the correct effect.

There is, however, one essential prerequisite for command over cinema craft. You must have a profound and judicious comprehension of the nature of the medium from an actor's point of view. I don't mean that a great actor should be able to engage in serious philosophical discussions about the place of cinema in a social democracy (we'll leave that to the critics); no, what he should have is a thorough grasp of the material resources of cinema and use these to establish his character for the audience.

Remember Nargis in *Barsaat* and the peculiar way she used to sniffle—well, I think that peculiarity managed to make her mountain girl portrait more memorable. Remember Anouk Aimee in *A Man and a Woman* and the casual way she used to flick her hair back—well, I think that flicker managed to add so much to her naturalness.

A great actress has a veritable Pandora's box. Inside this box you will find a wide storage of props from which she draws as and when required. As each day passes, the actress keeps adding new props to this box since even the greatest actress never stops learning.

If my heroine could summon tears to her eyes at will this is only one specimen of how professionally dexterous she was. This professionalism was corroborated for me by all the directors with whom she had worked and all of them to a man had enormous respect for my heroine as a craftsman. Homi Wadia, Gulzar, Abrar Alvi, Tak, Vijay Bhatt, Ralhan, Hrishikesh Mukherjee, Bimal Roy—all discovered that they seldom had to reshoot with Meena Kumari. The first take was the best take.

When she was signed up for *Char Dil Char Rahen* there was some problem with dates. My heroine could spare only fifteen days for this film due to a heavy schedule. Abbas was unhappy at the span allotted to him and wondered if he could complete the script in such a short time. Much to his delight he found those fifteen days were ample since, thanks to my heroine's professionalism, work progressed phenomenally fast. 'A sequence that would take four hours to shoot with any other heroine would take just ten minutes with Meenaji,' one of her directors told me.

How adept she was in using artifacts to help her is demonstrated by her application of concentrated Eau de Cologne under her nose for the second half of *Sahib Bibi Aur Ghulam*, in which she becomes an alcoholic. To the studio she would bring a large bottle of cologne and with a cloth dab it under her nose. The irritation produced by this allowed her to assume the drooping heavy look associated with immoderate consumption of liquor.

As a village widow in *Dushman* she is being taken in an open jeep to see the big factory. She sits not in the middle or to one side but on the absolute extreme—almost falling out of the vehicle. This intelligent positioning signifies to the audience without further elaboration how unused and frightened she is of the modern contraption.

We have not yet, in my view, come to the heart of great acting. You can have the best technical cunning, the most elastic physical medium, but it is the last Montague stipulation—a passion of joy in the character acted—around which the fate of great acting revolves. And here my heroine stands alone.

A word on this passion of joy. You can't fake it. You can't borrow it. You can't switch it on. It's either there or it isn't. The surfeit of indifferent and unconvincing performances on our screen today are, in my view, directly the result of acting dishonesty. Too many people are going around signing contracts without feeling the slightest affinity or interest in the character they have signed up to play. The time-honoured rule in acting, I always thought, was: never accept a part unless you feel seduced and drawn to it. Our matinee idols, I suppose, are not bothered by such trivialities.

It might interest these people to know the Herculean efforts real actors make to equip themselves mentally and physically for a role. George C. Scott prepared himself thus for *Patton*. He read thirteen biographies, watched old newsreels and watched them so often that they were completely worn out when he finally returned them, had his dentist mould him a set of caps to duplicate Patton's, shaved his head and wore a wig of white fuzz and filled in part of his nose to make it look more like the general's. That is what a passion of joy is all about and I am sure Meena Kumari would have matched Mr Scott's efforts had she been asked to play Patton, and had she accepted.

Fans say my heroine had fine sense of characterization, they say she identified herself utterly with the character she was portraying, they say she became the person she was creating, and celebrated this change. All very well and I suppose this is what Montague had in mind. But what fascinates and intrigues me is how she did it, did it repeatedly and then returned to her normal self.

We come at this point to the quintessence of what makes an actress great—what differentiates her from the simply pedestrian or the mediocre or the average or the competent. A great actress (or actor) is many human beings accommodated, not necessarily harmoniously, into one physical entity. In the case of my heroine there was a Hindu wife in her, there was a mother in her, there was a lover in her, there was a nurse in her, there was a prostitute in her, there was an elder sister in her, there was an alcoholic in her ... and whichever part of this make-up was required, she summoned that and became that. Meena Kumari was a kind of a personality prism through which she was able to project, with the aid of her tangible artistic skills, a variety of human beings all of equal veracity and plausibility.

Let my heroine speak for herself: 'I think unless an artiste feels the role, he or she cannot succeed in delineating it effectively. While enacting a particular character one has to replace "oneself". And the self-cultivated consciousness of being someone else is the foundation of great acting.'

So inflexible was this 'oneness' that she confessed, 'There are times when I became a total stranger to myself. This is all the more true when I see my own films. I get so lost sometimes that I forget I am the heroine and keep witnessing it as though it were any other film just as any filmgoer would do.'

Such perfection and devotion has its price. And Meena Kumari was perfectly aware of this. In fact, these are the hazards all great actors and actresses have to face. The more resolute and determined hang on, others have a nervous breakdown and chuck it in. This is how my heroine saw it, 'The hangover of portraying a tragic character lasts far longer than people normally imagine. I first recognized this feeling while I was acting *Anarkali* which Kamal Sahab was directing. In my childhood I had read this famous drama. It was written by the famous writer Imtiaz Ali Taj. I remembered the drama while enacting *Anarkali* on the screen and said to myself: Here I am portraying the feelings about which I had only read. The effect was remarkable. First time I felt I was merging my personality with my role. This feeling thrilled me, but I realized in later years that this "oneness" with the character leaves a shattering impact on one's personality and it haunts one for a considerable period of time. Such close identification with your role is no doubt the apex of histrionic art, but it has its own effects on your nerves, at times even on your health.' It says a lot for the courage and aesthetic integrity of my heroine that, knowing the perils, she was not in any way dissuaded, or in any way disposed to minimize the intensity of this 'oneness'.

Montague's passion was my heroine's passion and it glowed brilliantly in her fanatical, almost ecclesiastical loyalty to work. Safe to say, the one thing in her life that mattered above everything else was her work, and no sacrifices, private or professional, were too great in its perusal. Great art is hard work and the kind of zeal Meena Kumari showed towards her work is common to all great artistes. Picasso, ninety now, who works eighteen hours a day, was complaining in an interview of the necessity to sleep. He wished he could do without it so as to have more time to paint.

During the entire shooting of Mere Apne my heroine was stricken with temperature of 100 to 101 degrees. Yet she arrived on the set as scheduled. Invariably, she was too weak to walk since her legs were swollen, and Gulzar would help her. She would sit on her allotted chair and wait for the cue. 'When it came,' Gulzar said, 'there was a transformation. The woman that stood up and walked towards the camera was not the sick woman sitting on the chair. Instead, a new woman was visible—the old woman character of my film. You have to see it to believe it. As soon as the shot was over she was usually so exhausted that she would collapse back on to her chair. However, I did not once hear her complain about discomfort.'

When in sound health, this same devotion was present. On one of the days during the shooting of Abbas's film, there was an unusually heavy rainfall. Abbas was worried because he was sure his set would be all wet. So he got up early in the morning and went to the studio with his cameraman and junior director. They spent some time inspecting the set, trying to get it into shape. It was still raining at eight o'clock and Abbas looked at his watch, the sky, and remarked to his colleagues, 'I don't think the heroine will be coming today.' Just then a car came into the studio and a woman emerged. She got out, lifted her sari, walked through knee-deep water and nonchalantly entered into her make-up room. That woman was my heroine.

All this is nothing compared to what I am going to tell you next. After she came back from London in 1968, having received treatment, the doctors there strictly ordered her to resume her work gradually. They outlined a work chart and suggested that she should work no more than certain number of hours a week. She nodded her head then, but broke this work chart a week after she arrived back. Her physician here tried to stop her, her friends, sisters, colleagues told her to go easy, but she listened to none. Had she rested and followed the advice of her doctors she would have surely lived for a few more years. *Star and Style, Screen, Filmfare*, all say my heroine died because of her melancholy private life; I say she died because she couldn't stay away from the studios.

She was exceptionally quick to grab a part which excited her, and also tremendously sure of her material. A novice writer-director went to her home, shivering in his boots, with the purpose of engaging her for a film he had written. She asked him in with her customary politeness and he began reading his project. Halfway through she stopped him and said she would like a paan break. The leaf arrived, she chewed it thoughtfully for a minute and said, 'There is no need for you to continue reading any further. I have decided that I want the part you have in mind for me.' The writer was naturally delirious at his unexpected and prompt bounty and attempted to discuss terms and money with my heroine. She reprimanded him gently, 'If I like a script all that is of no consequence.'

I could give you so many illustrations of the lengths she went to arrive at identification and oneness with characters she was portraying. Here is one apt specimen. The day's shooting was in a quarry under the hot midday sun. It was a longish sequence and my heroine was playing the part of a barefoot labourer working in this quarry. Characteristically, when she came to work that day she was wearing nothing on her feet. The director suggested that this was not necessary and

ordered a pair of substitute chappals. He said she could take
them off when they came to the actual shooting. My heroine
said no. Since she was portraying a woman unable to afford
footwear, she should get a feel of what it is like to be such a
woman—hence it was essential to have the hot sun burning
under her soles.

If you have successfully made seventy-seven films (ignoring
the child films) in your life, you have to be a superhuman or a
robot to be consistently and uniformly great—and my heroine
was neither. She was influenced and affected by the people
and the kind of film she was working for. Almost always she
was associated with people and material that were abysmally
poor. Understandably, this atmosphere had repercussions
on the performances of my heroine. However, and this was
her saving grace, even when she was 'influenced' she was still
good enough. There was always a minimum level of artistry,
a standard below which she could never fall. Her second best
was more than adequate to humble all others on the screen who
appeared with her. Possibly this is a reflection on the health and
state of acting in an industry which prides itself in producing
the largest number of films in the world; and possibly this is a
reflection on how advanced an actress my heroine was.

Personally, I am convinced that there were at the outside
six to seven films in which Meena Kumari was fully stretched
as an artiste. The sixty-odd films she made otherwise, she
could have walked through with her eyes closed. For me, her
genius was established in her ability to achieve, even in the
most hackneyed and unimaginative parts, something different,
some new insight, some new assurance, some new reality, some
new meaning. Kenneth Tynan once remarked of Katherine
Hepburn, 'The parts she took were nearly unactable; yet she

took them, acted in them and found triumph in them.' Couldn't the same be said for my heroine?

Taking the last two decades of Hindi cinema where does my heroine stand? How does she compare with those who were her contemporaries? Part of my brief is to place Meena Kumari in the pantheon of Hindi film actresses. What measure of public popularity did she achieve? Was she No. 1?

Kamini Kaushal, Suraiya, Nimmi, Nutan, Vyjayanthimala —forces to be reckoned with in their days—did not stand the acid test of time. They came, they saw a modicum of acclaim and they went. My heroine survived. So that dismisses Vyjayanthimala, Kamini, Suraiya and Nimmi. Madhubala had admittedly a prettier face; what she lacked was Meena Kumari's range, intelligence and sensitivity. Waheeda Rehman, the only one of our present stock whose name can be taken in the company of my heroine, has a lot to learn, though I think she has potential enough to pose a threat to my heroine.

That leaves only Nargis, who, in the coveted hall of fame, fights for a place against Meena Kumari. But even Nargis, for reasons which are not entirely clear, cut short a brilliant career by self-imposed exile. In contrast my heroine dominated the cinema scene for twenty years and as such I feel she stands a little way ahead of Mrs Dutt.

What then is the Meena Kumari tragedy, the irreplaceable loss that all and sundry keep speaking about? Hadn't she at the age of forty achieved everything that an artiste can possibly wish to achieve? As an actress, was there anything left undone? I think not. Within the confines of the Bombay film studios she had got as far as she possibly could.

Maybe it is a good thing my heroine is no more. I don't think I could stand another film of hers, tears in eyes, praying in front of Hindu gods, begging for mercy or blessings. She would have been wasted on a cinema preoccupied with its trite ambitions. Who would have given her a chance at forty to play Chhoti Bahu or *Parineeta*'s Lalita.

Abbas, that incurable optimist, left me with an honourable idea. 'Had she lived, it is possible she could have inspired the more intelligent of our writers and directors to put together a film worthy of her talents. Now that she is gone, that source of inspiration is gone.' That is a beautiful thought and I won't add anything to it except that I don't believe it.

Time, finally, for an unambiguous verdict on Meena Kumari the artiste: She was easily the greatest, most accomplished film actress this country has produced in the last twenty years.

NINE

The Woman

Badi Bechari Hai
Meena Kumari
Jisko Lagi Hai
Dil Ki Bimari

(Poor Meena Kumari is indeed helpless for she is
suffering from an ailment of the heart)

— Meena Kumari

One of the less likeable interests of this country and its
populace is film stars. Their off-screen activities, their
on-screen activities, their marriages, love affairs, birthdays,
hobbies ... it would seem that the average Indian cannot get
enough of this kind of information.

This interest, although psychologically wasteful and possibly
reprehensible, has basis. Cinema, after all, is the only genuine
mass medium in this country and the film star, to a person who
leads an unexciting predictable life (most do), becomes a very
real person. He becomes a personification of the good life: of
glittering premiere shows, of late-night parties, of beautiful

178

women, of expensive imported cars. I have a strong feeling that if you conducted an 'opportunity poll' in India and asked the fifty-six crore population with whom they would like to change places most, fifty-five crore would answer 'film stars'. Why this should be is a question I am not equipped to answer. That is work cut out for a gigantic social scientist.

Not that the inhabitants of other lands are uninterested in their Rajesh Khannas and Mumtazs. Preoccupation with film stars is not an Indian peculiarity. The degree and intensity is. I mean I have never, in some of the countries I have travelled, had the privilege of overhearing the sort of partisan and animated conversation I heard some time ago in an Irani restaurant. Two contestants spent a good thirty minutes (possibly longer because when I left they were still at it) arguing the respective merits of M/s Shatrughan Sinha and Pran. Who was the more vicious-looking villain was the nucleus of the argument.

Perhaps Western man is too busy leading a full life. What with traffic jams, television, infidelities, there is little time for vicarious living. The point of departure between say an Indian and an American is that for the latter the film star is remote from life. He is a character who appears on the screen and then fades away. For the Indian, however, the character does not fade away at the end of the film. We bring him home into our sitting rooms and bedrooms. We put up his pictures on our walls (two things you will see in most homes are pictures of gods and film stars). We discuss, speculate, criticize and admire him, not so much for his professional acumen, but for the clothes he wears, the way he parts his hair, the affairs he is supposed to be having. His failures become our failures, his triumphs our triumphs.

Now I would be the first to concede that Mr Dev Anand

has a place and position in our society. He is certainly more important than a bus conductor and certainly less important than a primary schoolteacher. What we have lamentably failed to do is find for our film stars a status commensurate with their contribution to society. Instead, we have elevated them to such dizzy Himalayan heights that they themselves are frightened—because that same adulation turns to cold indifference once the star has tumbled off the popularity chart.

But if you live in downtown Barabanki how do you keep in touch with your favourites? Simple. You go to your nearest bookshop and whichever language you are adept in, you choose your reading matter. Not for nothing does India lead the world when it comes to film journals. In these you will find everything which ideally you should not find. As a bonus, colourful, big blow-ups are offered which you can remove conveniently and stick on your wall. For Re 1 or Rs 1.50 you can get all your choicest questions answered.

If you are looking for some perceptive prose on new trends in cinema or on the abilities of a particular actor, you will, chances are, be disappointed. However, if you wish to know why Shashi Kapoor keeps three of his shirt buttons open, you will, chances are, be rewarded.

The proprietors of these film magazines are clever people. Having sensed the inclination of their readers they deliberately and unashamedly cater to the lowest common denominator.

A very good example of this is a new English monthly called *Stardust*. In a perverse kind of way I admire it immensely, since it stimulates and satisfies an assortment of film scandals which, I suspect, people find unputdownable. Some samples: So-and-so is having a baby but the father's identity is unknown; so-and-so was dancing close with so-and-so's wife in a nightclub in

London (they've got spies everywhere); so-and-so got drunk at a party and had to be physically removed. There was always a streak of low gossip in our film mags but it was usually harmless. What *Stardust* has astutely done is to take it to the level of the gutter. If in the next few months this mag becomes a best-seller, it will be no coincidence.

For the writer of this biography these journals are at once a help and a hindrance.

Help because, thanks to them, I can assume that you have knowledge of my heroine. No doubt you've seen her films, but more, you've seen her 'pics' in these magazines, read the odd remark she may have made or an interview she may have given. This plus the staple gossip, of course. Now, since her death, you've absorbed the many generous obituaries which all set out to tell a 'Meena Kumari story'. I am not suggesting that this story or the magazine version is inaccurate or untrue. All I am saying is that you have not only an interest in my subject but additionally you are informed about it—which is a great help to me. (Have just finished reading the July issue of *Shama*, an Urdu monthly, and offhand there were at least a dozen letters from all over the country, from people who did not simply express grief but formulated a wide cross section of opinion on my heroine as a person. The letters had one thing in common: they were all remarkably well informed, and showed a grasp of detail which I am sure was the result of avid film mag reading.)

Hindrance, because cumulatively these magazines have stabilized an image (I shall examine it just now) in your mind. You may have added something to this model or subtracted from it, but you have at this moment a well-defined mental picture of my heroine. It is possible that in the course of my appraisal of the human being Meena Kumari, I may tarnish or further whiten this image. The latter poses no problems, the former does. If I refer to certain conventionally disagreeable but human aspects of my heroine, hitherto unrevealed, and if some of these tell a different story, you could be forced to re-examine your existing image. Now, nobody likes to be told he is wrong, that he has been a trifle gullible. In short, I might lose your sympathy and your ear. But, I feel I would be grievously failing in my duty if I did not attempt to tell the truth about my heroine on the basis of my own investigations and on the basis of my own judgement.

Let me present the image you had, and even I had, before I started this book, of Meena Kumari the person separate from the actress. I think it was essentially a sad one: of a lonely, dejected, unloved, suffering person who found great artistic satisfaction, but slight personal joy. Bereft of parental love and happy family life she rose from the very low only to discover the rightness of the cruel maxim that money cannot buy happiness.

We are told she loved extravagantly and recklessly, but the people she bestowed this love on exploited and deceived her. Precisely this point was made in all the magazine versions of Meena Kumari: 'Many people exploited Meena Kumari. There are people who exploited her financially. Worse, there are even people who used her physically and exploited her emotionally, leaving indelible wounds on her heart.'

Her marriage was a well-publicized failure. Mr Amrohi, they say, was not a good husband, though Mr Amrohi claims he was a good husband, but that my heroine's kinsmen were bad relatives and sabotaged his wedlock. Whatever, the marriage was a failure.

Then there were the men in her life, among whom Dharmendra was No. 1 and typical. He too, it appears, used my heroine to establish himself in the eyes of producers and, once this was accomplished, speedily left.

The move to the bottle was logical and almost necessary. You probably know that Meena Kumari, in order to forget and drown her sorrows, took to drink, and drank so uncaringly that she died of it.

Kindness and sensitivity are two other aspects you are familiar with. Everybody who met my heroine made good, received some bounty—'her touch was the touch of gold,' said Sawan Kumar Tak who had enjoyed the touch. Her sensitivity can be seen in her poems, in her literary interests, in her serene and phlegmatic nature. *Filmworld*, I thought, summed up the official version best: 'She remained in the mid-ocean just looking at the horizon, never crossing it. The only happiness she found was in the fatal kiss of death, when God took her into his bosom to grant her eternal peace and bliss.'

Now give or take a little, this is the kind of composite picture you have of Meena Kumari. And it is indeed a wretched one. Gulzar kept telling me of the 'aura of melancholy' which always hung around her and it is easy to see why. Every possible mortal misery it seems visited Meena Kumari who martyr-like endured it all.

Life was persecution and anguish and she described it as such in one of her poems: 'Wounds, turmoils, defeats, constant companions of my heart.' Or more dramatically, '*Jaise Jaagi Hui Aankhon Mein Chubhen Kaanch Ke Khwab, Raat Is Tarah Deewanon Ki Basar Hoti Hai*' (The way dreams made out of glass prick wide-awake eyes, that is how some people spend the night).

Why does this image make me restless? Why do I find it

difficult to accept the way it is offered? I suppose the world is full of Meena Kumaris—people who seem to get more than their allotted share of problems and difficulties. In my very limited experience of life I have met a few women who could match my heroine for sorrow. No, what makes me restless is the Meena Kumari story. It is too much like an Indian film (and we know how real they are). There are the good guys and the bad guys, there is love briefly happy, there is melodrama, there is alcohol, and there is the final tragedy.

One more thing. The Meena Kumari fable I have outlined above makes my heroine out to be a mighty martyr—someone who suffered the slings and arrows of outrageous fortune uncomplainingly—and to put it at its most indelicate, a rather silly martyr. A woman who willingly allowed herself to be used, exploited, betrayed, duped, time and time again. Was she that unworldly? Was she really a silly martyr? I can tell you one thing, in advance: the magazine version of my heroine is not only sloppy, but an insult to her intelligence.

Listen to my version.

Mammon usually tells character. You can, I believe, estimate the mettle of an individual by his attitude to paper money. Now the Bombay film star is about as magnanimous as a bankrupt Shylock. In his list of priorities money comes much before art. Some months ago the nation watched with amused interest the dacoit-like raids of the Internal Revenue Department on the establishments of 'respected names' in our cinema industry. Flats were broken into, safes were smashed, walls demolished, grounds dug up in an effort to excavate the 'Black Money' which everybody knows is the standard mode of payment in the industry. I can never understand how anybody who has the temerity to call himself an artiste, and who makes loud noises about his dedication to the profession, can find the time and mental apparatus to handle and organize the tortuous deceits necessary for hoarding hot money. If you have ten lakh rupees hidden under your bathroom sink, how in God's name can you concentrate in front of the camera?

It would be very nice if I could state categorically that Meena Kumari's contracts were strictly legal. Given the nature of capitalism, those who signed and sealed deals on her behalf made sure that the 'black/white' requisite was clearly understood. I am convinced that she was aware of these deals, but, redeemingly, she took not the slightest interest in their progress. The sordid commercial transactions of her talent did not consume a second of her time.

Mind you, Meena Kumari was a woman who knew the value and worth of a paisa. By birth she was not accustomed to money, or accustomed to spending it in large amounts, and if she had directed her life to the pursuit of wealth, one could have forgiven her. But she did not.

Surprisingly and refreshingly, she was a lady of nearly foolish generosity. To begin with she had no head for money. (As is their wont, our producers frequently paid my heroine in large bundles. She would never count these and always asked someone else to do it for her.) In the early years of her life, while her father was still alive, the financial matters and accounts were entrusted to him. Later, when she married Kamal Amrohi he took on the job of banker. In the concluding portion of her life she was short of liquid cash and a little tight. Otherwise, till about 1968 she didn't give a damn about a dime. There were for her many other more rewarding and worthwhile things than bundles of 100-rupee notes.

What, one may well ask, is the meaning of generosity relative to a person who earns fifteen lakhs a year. (A conservative estimate of my heroine's income during her heyday.) When I went on my rounds talking to people, nearly all of them had some piquant story to tell of Meena Kumari's large-heartedness. I would ask myself: Did it really matter? Did it lighten her purse in any way if she advanced a thousand rupees to someone who came to her with a sob story?

And doesn't philanthropy help the donor more than the recipient? I used to make this point with great relish to my English friends when they went on about their contributions to charities like 'Oxfam' and 'War on Want'. Giving money gives one a glow of self-righteousness, it makes you feel good inside. Invariably, it is the most unscrupulous and corrupt businessman who hosts the most expensive 'kathas' and poojas.

Meena Kumari's generosity was of a different genre. She did not just feel 'good' when she loosened her purse since she was one of that rare breed who was large-hearted because she believed that if you have surplus, you should give.

Giving is good, giving with dignity is even better. I know. I was coming in a taxi a few nights ago, well stuffed. At a traffic stop I was accosted by a particularly pathetic beggar. He kept knocking on the taxi window and I frantically searched for some loose change to get rid of him. But the smallest change I had was a one-rupee note—and I wasn't going to alm that. So I reluctantly borrowed a ten-paisa coin from the driver, and by this time I had lost my cool. I was cursing the beggar for having ruined an otherwise idyllic evening.

My heroine was not like me. She gave with style and gave with cunning. She once approached a producer and requested him if he could give one of her relatives a small part in his forthcoming film.

The producer agreed.

'How much would you normally pay for that kind of part?' she asked.

'Rs 500,' he replied.

'Well, give him Rs 2,000,' she said, 'I'll make up the difference.'

Meena Kumari could easily have given this handout to the relative in question. But she appreciated that her relative would have more respect for himself if he felt he had earned the money. She knew, and here the quality of her generosity blazes out, that one can be generous, that one can give someone Rs 1,500, but one can also in the process humble and humiliate a person, make him grovel on the ground.

Khwaja Ahmed Abbas was short of money. He had started a film and had run out of funds halfway through. In order to raise collateral he wrote to all his friends. My heroine heard of this fund-raising scheme and promptly rang up Abbas.

'So you don't think I am your friend,' she complained.

'Why do you say that?' he asked.

'Well, you wrote to all your friends for money but not me.'

Then it was a joke and they both laughed over the telephone.

The next day a cheque of 5,000 rupees signed by my heroine arrived at Abbas's house. He accepted it gratefully and when finally he was in a position to pay back, he went with the money to my heroine's house. 'This is the first time someone is repaying me a loan,' she chuckled.

The example of her unselfishness I like most concerns Kamal Amrohi and *Pakeezah*. In a letter she wrote to her husband in early 1969 she said, 'In regard to my working in *Pakeezah*, I have always been willing and clamouring to work. *Pakeezah* is my life dream and it will be my greatest pleasure to see it completed. As for my remuneration, I am glad you have given me an opportunity to prove my regards and respect for you. I shall accept only ONE GUINEA as a token of goodwill for my entire work in *Pakeezah*.' If this is not contempt for money I don't know what it is.

We live in mercenary times. Times in which generosity means money. So when we say Meena Kumari was a generous person we automatically conjure up visions of a woman who parted money with ease. By all accounts this measurement is both cheap and insufficient in reference to my heroine. I would like to talk of Meena Kumari's generosity of spirit: the way she would bid welcome to people into her house, the way she would listen to people reciting their troubles, the way she would conduct herself on the sets, the way she would suffer fools, the way she would treat people like me (journalists). Perhaps these are minor considerations of etiquette and old-world protocol, yet they are so rare these days to be almost extinct.

The Bombay cinema anyway was never a serious candidate in the humanity stakes. Its inhabitants are mostly brusque, egocentric, very often rude individuals. One understands their problems. One understands the pressure on their lives. One understands they have to meet literally hundreds of people each single day. But how come my heroine, thirty-six years in this world, remained untainted? How come till her last breath she remained supremely a decent human being?

I think back to a conversation I had with her make-up man. He had been serving her for nearly ten years. We sat quietly one evening in my flat. 'Please tell me something about Meena Kumari?' I asked. He began a non-stop two-hour monologue, and by the time he had finished he had tears in his eyes. For him she was nothing short of a goddess. I don't think I shall forget what he said to me as we parted, 'Please write a good book about her.' He made this statement with such simple and direct poignancy that I could only mumble something to the effect that I would try.

How did she manage to extract such devotion, such esteem? I can quite understand directors and co-stars having respect for her because of her artistic genius, but how did she manage to get the same devotion from the tea boy at the studio?

Primarily, because she took an unheard-of interest in everybody around her. The cameraman, production assistant, lighting incharge, canteen king, were all known to her. A visitor who watched her working was surprised at her familiarity with names of the most insignificant studio staff. A little thing, but even when she asked for a glass of water she would say, 'Shanker ...'

You can imagine how Shanker felt. Here was possibly the greatest star in India and she was on first-name terms with him, the water-man.

Someone once asked her how she managed to remember all the names of the studio staff. 'It's hard work. However it is easier than remembering the dialogue lines.'

Interest was not restricted to glasses of water. Shanker and hundreds like him discovered, much to their amazement and delight, that my heroine's concern in their personal fortunes was deep and consistent. 'How is your son? How is your wife? Have you moved to your new house yet? I believe you were unwell. Are you feeling better now?' This was the sort of interest she had in the Shankers of the studio world. They in turn called her 'Meena Didi' and when she would arrive at the set I am told there was a general lifting of the atmosphere.

Abbas's *Naya Sansar* Unit used to call her their 'No. 1
heroine' and such was her interest in the welfare of the unit
that she was asked, 'Whom are you in love with in *Naya Sansar?*'
Her reply was typical, 'With the whole unit.'

She always found time to listen to other people's woes.
This attribute I find particularly perplexing because she had
such a collection of woes of her own. I wonder why she
didn't ever revolt hearing Shanker's problems. Had she been
an inordinately happy person I could have understood, but
considering her perilous personal state this propensity is indeed
remarkable and praiseworthy.

Naturally, the word quickly spread that Meena Didi was
'simpatica'. Not only did she listen and advise, but she helped
materially in whatever way she could. By the time she died,
my heroine had become the Meena Didi of nearly all the
Bombay studios.

I think I can understand her make-up man's devotion. It
seems he called her once to his house, not in Malabar Hill
but in Foras Road, to attend some function. His colleagues
warned him and laughed. 'She won't come,' they all said. Not
only did she come, she also mingled with the crowd, stayed
for two hours and was perfectly at ease.

One other quality, in association with her generosity, I must
touch on. It is a very underrated quality and unfortunately
not many people appreciate its importance. Meena Kumari
had a unique knack for listening. When you spoke to her,
irrespective of who you were, she was all attention. 'She
waited on every word you uttered,' Abrar Alvi told me, 'added
meaning to even the most mundane remark you made in her
presence.' Oh, I know this is a public relations trick, but what
a beautiful trick.

My heroine seldom lost her temper or blew her cool. I have lately been studying the temperaments of great actors and actresses. Mostly they are hot-headed, neurotic, ignitable individuals. Rod Steiger is impossible to work with, James Dean frequently boxed with his director. Nicol Williamson engenders such fury that no one comes near him.

My heroine's equanimity like most other things was legendary. Unruffled, unperturbed she would arrive at work completely prepared. I believe Mr Dilip Kumar requires that the set be cleared when he is playing an important scene; not Meena Kumari. 'I am an actress,' she told a director, 'I should be able to work anywhere, any time.' I bring this up because this is another illustration of her willingness to be treated on the set at par with the most humble. No special privileges for India's foremost tragedienne were required.

One of the film magazines rang her up for an interview. She agreed and asked that the interviewer be sent to the studio. The interviewer arrived and went looking all over the set for her but couldn't locate her. Finally he gave up and asked one of the studio staff to help him find Meena Kumari. 'She is sitting directly opposite you,' he was told. And sure enough she was sitting on the floor with a group of extras drinking tea in a glass and having a great time. Reminds me of those lovely Kipling lines: 'If you can walk with Kings yet keep the common touch ...'

So far so good, but my heroine had flaws too.

Chief among them was her weakness for self-pity. Somehow she had come to the conclusion that she was uniquely unfortunate and had been hand-picked by fate to bear every conceivable domestic misfortune. And she indulged this self-pity in sometimes morbid and irresolute ways.

The world, she believed, was determined to inflict on her injuries, and Meena was determined to demonstrate to this world that she had a fakir's capacity for suffering these inflictions. In some ways she was contesting with what she thought to be her fate: 'Show me your worst cruelties and I will show you my best phlegm.' Inside my heroine a small masochist was trying to get out.

This yearning after the melancholy, this streak of masochism was directly connected with her professional status. I am convinced that had Meena Kumari not been a film star but just an average Sunni or Shia wife she would have been a much happier person—because what was largely responsible for destroying her was her cinema image. Yes, that grand tragedienne crap which you and I shamelessly encouraged in the form of acclaim and requests for autographed photographs.

Thirty-six out of her forty-year life, Meena Kumari was doused in grease paint—playing one tragedy after another: crying and dying, raped and molested, widowed and betrayed. How many frames can you remember of a smiling Meena? 'I have known nothing but work and work. Bright studio lights that are with me even in my dreams, and I am conscious of the ever-present mike even when I indulge in harmless conversation,' she said in a rare admission.

This ever-present mike by 1954 or 1955 had shouted to the entire nation that my heroine was unbeatable when it came to personifying misery. And slowly but surely she herself became convinced that misery was going to be her life—private and professional. The former was a most unfortunate conclusion.

Another interesting irony: had Meena Kumari been a less accomplished actress she would probably have been saved;

but she identified so closely with her roles, played them with such immaculate tear-rending perfection that she was unable to switch off once the cinema lights had been extinguished.

Discussing my heroine the actress in the earlier section I highlighted one of the dangers of great acting: the inability of some performers to regain their intrinsic personalities after portraying make-believe personalities. Meena Kumari was one such performer.

The great tragedienne Meena Kumari became the great tragedienne not only in front of the cinema but behind it. And this is the real sorrow, she aided the latter. Some devil inside her whispered, 'You must project this mantle of melancholy everywhere you go, otherwise your fans won't believe your screen persona.'

Therefore the masterly inactivity. Therefore the martyr-like stance. Therefore the stoic.

Meena Kumari was neither a gullible human being nor a stupid human being, nor a seven-year-old human being. On the contrary, she was perfectly and painfully aware that she was surrounded by sharks, pimps, profiteers who had not the slightest sympathy in her welfare. But she told herself that she was the unfortunate one, that she was born to be exploited, that this was all part of being the great tragedienne.

Now there is absolutely no doubt in my mind—despite protestations of innocence from all I met—that my heroine was used financially by all: sisters, relatives, friends, lovers, husband, secretaries, all. These people gave her blank pieces of papers to sign, refused to return money she had deposited, cooked the account books ... she knew all this and yet she did nothing.

A story she herself recounts concerns a young man who

had come to see her at Landmark when she was ill. He was all concern. Oh, how sorry he was at her illness. As soon as he heard he had come running. Listening to all this Meena knew that the concern was phony. The young man had come because he had some favour to ask—and just before he left he did.

If only she had kicked this young man, and hundreds like him, in the pants. Enough is enough, I wish she said.

After all, Meena Kumari was not the only popular film star of Bombay. The pressures that she was subject to were in no way exclusive. A little resolution and determination and she would have conquered them.

In a brief conversation Nargis mentioned how heartlessly Meena had been used. I agreed, but wasn't she in the ideal world for exploitation?

Hrishikesh Mukherjee made a film sometime ago (*Guddi*) in which he tried to depict cinema life as it really exists. Mr Mukherjee is an honest and intelligent man but his version was so soft, so respectful, so glib, that it was almost untrue.

Meena Kumari was a gift to all the conniving, unscrupulous manipulators in the Bombay studios. You can't imagine how sordid the transactions of the cinema industry are and you can't imagine how many just hang about hoping to make a fast buck: the friends of stars, the people who 'got things done', the full-time sycophants. My heroine was the perfect sucker for such people and these parasites buzzed round her.

One jerk, one slap and she could have got rid of them—but she did not, and here we come back to my earlier hypothesis: my heroine felt this constantly being had was necessary if her public tragedienne photo was to be sustained and strengthened.

Self-pity thus was a natural manifestation of this life. Towards 1964 it got so bad that if you wished to win Meena's sympathy all you had to say was, 'Meenaji, you are really a very unfortunate person.'

In defence of Meena Kumari I must state, without an iota of doubt, that she was not congenitally self-pitying. There was nothing in the genes she inherited from Ali Bux or Iqbal which cultivated deep dejection—it was just those damn *Filmfare* awards.

The temptation is great, I know. The press almost to a person has lifted its finger and pointed to all of us as conspirators and contributors in the assassination of Meena Kumari. People like you and me, they say, killed her.

This theory of 'collective guilt' makes good copy but precious else. It is also inaccurate and naive.

Every single actor in this film jungle of ours designs and develops his own defence mechanisms, his own suit of armour. By getting inside this suit he wards off the kind of attacks all favourite stars have to face. My heroine failed to design her shield and like a larger version of Achilles left herself wide open. And, this is very significant, left herself wide open by choice.

Gulzar mentioned to me many times how sensitive a person Meenaji was. In fact he came up with a rather ingenious explanation which goes something like: Meena Kumari the poetess, the admirer of Faiz and Mir, the lover of flowers and sea stones did not have the brain to defend herself against the onslaughts of her attackers.

I find this difficult to accept. I yield to no one in my respect for my heroine's sensitivity (and, incidentally, sensitivity doesn't mean you are a moron) but despite that, I think she was a shrewd, worldly person with both feet firmly on the ground.

As far as exploitation (financial) is concerned my view is that Meena Kumari was to a large measure herself responsible for her adversity.

This is possibly not the best place but I would like to include my heroine's poetic manifestations here. Like Dr Johnson she believed that the purpose of poetry is to 'better enjoy life or better to endure it'.

Writing under the 'Thakalos' (pen-name) of *Naaz*, Meena Kumari was a fairly prolific poet. I have in my possession an LP of her poems and a book published by Mr Gulzar.

One of my heroine's passions in life was Urdu poetry, and as I mentioned earlier, she spent most of her leisure hours engrossed in the works of Mir, Jigar, Faiz, Sardar Jafri, Firaq. Herself, she started writing seriously in Janki Kutir and continued till the very last.

Although a Lucknow-refined philistine Punjabi, I am not really qualified to pronounce on the merits of *Naaz*. Fortunately, however, none of her renderings are complex or metaphysical and most of her work is within my grasp.

But let me first give you the opinion of the pundits. Gulzar considers that Meena Kumari's sense of imagery is very strong and vivid. Abbas considers her 'not a very good or deep poet'. Mr Amrohi considers her totally ignorant of all that poetry is about. Further opinions from established literary mouths all indicate that Meena Kumari was no Mirza Ghalib.

Her greatest virtue for me is that she wrote poetry at all. Remember she was employed in a profession where the literacy rate is not very high, and those on its payroll read nothing more taxing than *Cine Advance*. That she was able to put pen to paper in this sort of environment deserves a thirty-one-gun salute.

Poets write because they have something to say on the

human condition. They also write because they wish to engage in dialogue with themselves. Meena Kumari wrote because she had something to say, and because she wanted to talk to herself.

One other reason, perhaps a minor one: my heroine loved the concept of poetry—especially Urdu poetry. And what she was especially enamoured by were the atmospherics of this poetry.

Coming from Lucknow I know a little bit about these. The drink, the small participatory gathering (mehfil), the midnight hour, the showmanship, the elevated white dais, the elegant paan daan … this is what she loved.

For Mr Amrohi my heroine may not be good enough but for me she is. I relish her poetry. The accusation against her is that in her literary efforts Meena was selfishly self-absorbed, harping on the defeats and anguish of love, and the excruciating pain of loneliness. I don't know whether my Meena appreciated this, but in her poetry, however inadequate, she was expressing the oldest lover's lament. From Shakespeare to Shelley, from Goethe to Ghalib, from Auden to Lowell, poets have all spent lifetimes trying to pierce this curious phenomenon called 'love'. My heroine is in good company.

Her poetry is sad, joyless, pessimistic, morbid—but then what do you expect from a woman of the temperament of Meena Kumari? Her verses were entirely in character with her life, or at least her comprehension of her life. My heroine was not an outstanding poet, nor a detached poet, nor a penetrating poet, nor a classical poet. She was a learning poet who translated her life into verse.

All right, she was a third-rate poet. But does Rakhee write poetry? Does Hema Malini write poetry? Does Sharmila Tagore write poetry? Did Vyjayanthimala write poetry? Meena

Kumari was not only the greatest actress in the last twenty years, she was also the most literate.

The dominant strain in Meena Kumari's poetry is love, or rather the impossibility of finding love. And it would be true to say that my heroine looked and searched, wept and cried in its pursuit. 'In fact,' she said, 'love is my biggest weakness—and greatest strength too. I am in love with love. I am craving for love. I have been craving for it since my childhood.' We all know she was unsuccessful. One way, possibly the only way, to understand why she was unsuccessful is to search the places she searched.

The first and in my view the most crucial place is Rembrandt. Kamal Amrohi was the husband for twenty years and he was 'the man of her life' (not discounting Dharmendra, but he must take second place after Amrohi).

The Chandan-Manju marriage was a failure—one of the biggest in the film industry (I am just stating a fact, not apportioning blame). As I explored its causes I was given, substantially, both the Manju side and the Chandan side.

Khursheed, the eldest sister, catalogued a long series of Amrohi 'zulms' (cruelties). He beat her, underfed her, took her money, never made her a mother, kept her locked up in a cage. When she could take no more of these zulms my heroine packed her bags and left.

Meena, Khursheed says, was a most uncomplaining person and she refused to discuss her marital difficulties with anyone. She had a great capacity for endurance and for twelve years she took Amrohi's inhumanities without a word of protest.

Mr Amrohi naturally denies every single zulm. Instead, he says, he was an understanding and super-tolerant husband. 'I am a writer and a poet and I loved Manju with the passion and intensity of a poet. Can you imagine such a person being cruel?' he pleaded.

Let us examine the money bit first. Did my heroine leave because her Chandan was stealing her earnings?

That the husband made money even the husband does not deny. As he explained, 'After all she was my wife.' Since Meena and Kamal were living together, and since Kamal was controlling her finances, he certainly kept some by. My heroine was not a woman of expensive tastes or given to any show of luxury, and there was undeniably a bit left over each month.

How much he made no one can be certain. The sisters claim that Amrohi profited to the tune of rupees seventy-five to eighty lakhs. My researches lead me to believe it was much less. Meena Kumari in the early and late 1950s was earning no more than one and a half lakhs and it was only in 1963 that she signed her first five-lakh contract. Unquestionably, he made good, but then so did everybody else.

Did he not even give her pocket money? Did he keep her in rags? I don't think so. Amrohi says that bills worth Rs 600 were paid to Sahib Singhs nearly each month for the 'imported' cosmetics that Meena used. According to him, her wardrobe was full, expensive and new.

Continually, he says, he kept telling his wife that everything at Rembrandt belonged to her. She was the master and she could take what she wanted when she wanted. The rumour of her poverty was taken out by the 'Chandawallas', those people who make rounds of film star houses soliciting money for allegedly charitable causes. These folks said that when they called on my heroine to collect, she was very sympathetic but unable to give, since she had nothing—not even ten rupees.

One thing is definite: while she was with Amrohi, those

around her—and they were not only her relatives—were
deprived. And these were precisely the people who most resented
Amrohi's good fortune in landing the 'moneymaking machine'.

Many came for alms to her. First they would ask Amrohi
and he would invariably point to his wife's room. 'If you want
a loan please ask Manju. If she agrees you can have as much
as you like.'

Even if all this is untrue, even if Amrohi did make seventy-
five lakhs, the point to bear in mind is that my heroine was
about as keen on money as an Eskimo would have been on a
frigidaire. Literally she would recoil at the sight of bundled-up
notes. She played with wealth, joked with it and spurned it.
(One day she asked Amrohi for a monthly salary. He asked
her how much she wanted: 10,000, 5,000. 'No,' she said, 'I
want only hundred rupees.')

Among the causes of Meena Kumari's exodus from
Rembrandt money must figure very low.

Possibly a more plausible reason was that Chandan never
gifted her a child—or at least this, they say, was Meena's
complaint.

Most of those connected with my heroine confirm that she
loved and liked and adored little children. In the later part of
her life, Nargis relates how she once questioned Meena.

'Haven't you ever wanted to become a mother?'

'Is there any woman who does not want to become a mother,'
Meena replied with tears in her eyes.

Examples of Meena's fondness for children are numerous.

In Madras in 1961 she became great friends with Nargis (a
friendship that was unbroken till her death). Sunil was working
with Meena and they were all staying in the same hotel.

One evening Mr and Mrs Dutt invited my heroine for a

Chinese dinner. They said they had a table booked. She said she had been working very hard and would prefer an early night. But even the Dutts had problems: who was going to mind their two kids? There were no nannies in the hotel and a late-night Chinese meal was not a good habit to inculcate in the so young. Meena stepped in and offered to mind the children while Mr and Mrs Dutt ate chop suey.

Before midnight, when they returned to their rooms they found the children missing. Nargis tiptoed into my heroine's chamber and saw her two infants sleeping soundly with Meena on her bed.

While the parents were out, the children had received personal and devoted hospitality from my heroine. She washed them and cleaned them, helped them into their nightsuits, organized their milk, and finally induced them to sleep with a lullaby.

For child artistes on the sets, for her nieces and nephews, for the offspring of her friends, Meena showed similar concern. Khursheed explained clearly, 'She simply loved children. Kamal Sahab never wanted a child from Meena because he always felt superior to her and considered her nothing more than a cheap dancer's daughter.' Kamal Sahab, it is true, is a 'Sayyed'—the elite among the Shias—and my heroine was much lower to him in the social strata.

Twice though, with his aid, she was on the verge of motherhood. On both occasions she was unmothered.

They say he told her that having a child would be bad for her image. Her glamour as a heroine would be considerably diminished if her fans knew that she had babies to look after at home. Meena Kumari the woman must make this sacrifice for Meena Kumari the actress.

So powerful were these arguments that my heroine agreed, and the first attempt at motherhood was effectively scotched.

The second attempt, Meena's sympathizers continue, was doomed because of the first. Due to a faulty first abortion the second one turned septic and this time an operation wasn't desirable but vital.

As you have probably guessed, the husband has powerful arguments on his side too. 'If I could bring her into my home as my wife don't you think I would have been proud to have a child from her?' And then he turned the story on its head. Kamal said he would have been honoured with a child from Manju, but it was Manju who never wanted a baby.

'Why?' I asked.

'Because she felt it would harm her screen image.'

The first time she got in the family way, Amrohi says, he was out of town. When he came back he discovered her pale and sick. A few days later this worsened and he took her to the doctor, who after examining Meena told Amrohi privately that what he had brought was an abortion case, and what his wife was suffering from were the after-effects. Additionally, the doctor reprimanded Amrohi. If he didn't want his wife to have this child he should have gone about it properly and not used indigenous methods. Amrohi says he listened quietly and took all the doctor's scolding.

Meena later told him how she had bribed her 'massage woman' to do the deed.

A year later when Meena was again expecting, her womb became septic and it had to be aborted, Amrohi told me. The doctor also advised him that due to these two previous happenings it might be medically dangerous for his wife to

conceive and give birth. He recommended that they have no
children. Subsequently, Kamal says, 'We used to look at the
calendar.'

Two stories, both very convincing—but who is telling the
truth?

It's correct that a star's image is affected by too pronounced
a family life. It's also correct that if Amrohi's sole purpose in
marrying my heroine was to make money, he had an interest
in not becoming a father. (I am ignoring the lower-caste
aspect.)

The only person who knows the truth is not here, and
although it is part of my brief to sift facts and exercise my
judgement when the truth seems to clash, I cannot vouch for
either story. Facts I can confirm, but not motives, and the facts
are these: On two occasions my heroine was nearly a mother
and on both these occasions things were done to prevent her
from becoming one.

Of all the alleged zulms the one I heard from many mouths
was the one concerning physical violence. One of the sisters
in fact told me that she had seen this 'with my own eyes'. If
violence had not taken place, why should Meena have gone
to the police station on 5 March 1964 and reported that her
life was in danger, was a question posed to me.

The thinking is that when Amrohi married my heroine she
was an uninformed, submissive little woman. As she grew in
stature, however, she turned progressively more emancipated
in her ideas and actions. Kamal had not reckoned for this.
Being an old-fashioned husband he expected total obedience
from his wife, and more, he expected her to understand her
position vis-à-vis an Indian housewife.

So when my heroine 'answered back', as she frequently did,

to her husband, he was shocked and annoyed, and he took punitive action.

Mr Amrohi's position on this charge relies again on his love for his wife theme. He loved her, he says, like a poet loves a vision, and as far as he was concerned Manju could do nothing wrong. And if she did, he quickly forgave her because she was Manju.

The only bit of squabbling he has publicly acknowledged is the Eid incident, and if his version of that incident is faithful, he was certainly provoked.

'You know we are Sayyeds, and among us it is considered uncultured even to speak harshly to women. Beating them or hitting them is out of the question,' explained one of Kamal's aides. They maintain that my heroine herself, consciously or unconsciously, was responsible for circulating the 'Amrohi beats me' fable.

One example:

It appears, during one of her bad moods, while sitting at the dining table, she took a bottle and banged it against her head. It was a minor accident but it left a visible ugly scar on the forehead. When she went to the studio the next day people asked her, 'Meenaji, how did you get that scar?' Rather than giving a direct answer, Meena smiled equivocally and the questioners (already aware of rumours) were convinced that the perpetrator of this mark was none other than her husband.

However Mr Amrohi may argue, one thing is incontestable: Meena felt restricted and curtailed in Rembrandt. 'Bird in a cage' is possibly too emotive an expression and 'Bird in a house' is possibly more accurate.

First of all, there were the physical restrictions—the back home by 6.30, no one in the make-up room routine—which

greatly oppressed her. There is no record of my heroine
publicly protesting against her husband's curbs, but I am
positive she resented every single one of them.

At work her movements were watched and reported back
to the husband. 'Whose car did you sit in today?' No wonder
she turned paranoid.

Secondly, as an individual she began feeling thwarted
and concluded that in Rembrandt her colourful, distinctive
personality was being suppressed, indeed manipulated.

In short she was not prepared to be a meek, subservient
wife. She had her own interests and she was going to pursue
these in a manner she thought fit.

Freedom, then, was what Manju was looking for, and
freedom is what she did not get at Chandan's house.

What were Meena's real feelings for Kamal? This is the
vexing question which has perplexed and dodged me. What
happened to all that love she wrote so feelingly about in 1952
('My ideal man, etc.'). Did Amrohi's zulms alienate her to
such an extent that love turned to hatred? Or did she see her
entire marriage as a gigantic mistake, a hasty step taken by a
twenty-year-old girl?

For myself, I think she loved him no more than two years,
and then with each passing day she went further away. Why
she continued to live in Rembrandt so long makes no sense.
The move Meena made in 1964 could quite easily have been
made in 1960 or even earlier.

No doubt by 1964 Manju felt grievously towards her
Chandan, and she too tormented him, teased him and caused
him pain.

Curiously, she never said anything against him to her friends
or relatives or colleagues. She always spoke of him as 'Kamal

Sahab' and showed correct respect and reverence. The effect of this was that Amrohi became an even bigger criminal in the eyes of those watching; since all these people knew the real goings-on at Pali Hill, they credited my heroine with perhaps undeserved nobility and forgiveness.

It was on her part a master move. Had she openly quarrelled with Amrohi, her quantity of sympathy would have considerably lessened, and further it would have given Amrohi a chance to make his case, whatever its merits.

Cleverly, she kept up her side and insisted that she still loved Amrohi. Actually, with minor traces of malice, she made him run around in circles.

On the one hand, just before she went into the hospital for the last time, she commanded her sister not to inform Amrohi. Remember she was mortally ill and she knew it. Therefore the conclusion must be that she was prepared to see everybody else during her last days except her husband. However, when he came to the hospital she innocently got inside his embrace and declared, 'Chandan, I want to die in your arms.'

Chandan loved her I think. Loved her in his mad, misguided, possessing, Victorian way. I am even tempted to believe that for him she was a vision.

Today, however, he is a bitter man. He can forgive his Manju many things, he told me, but leaving her diaries to Gulzar is another matter. 'I never wanted her money or her riches, but those diaries morally belong to me because they contain so much of our private life. How did she have the heart to give them away?'

My heroine, as you probably know, bequeathed her diaries to Mr Gulzar in her will which she made out fifteen days before her death. And she left the option open to him whether to publish or not (already in a Meena Kumari issue of *Madhuri* pages from these diaries have been released).

I remember vividly an evening I spent with Amrohi. He was particularly agitated that day. 'People die. Gandhiji died, but Meena's death story seems to have no end.' The newspapers had finally got him. In one way or another they had all branded him as the villain. 'Please save me from these journalists,' he requested me.

'Because of Meena nobody talks to me in the film line. Everybody thinks I am a tyrant who killed her. Because of Meena I am today accused of all kinds of unspeakable crimes. But these people seem to forget that she left me in 1964 and she died in 1972. So something must have happened in the intervening eight years. Why don't they accuse those people who gave her "tharra" in whisky bottles? Why don't they accuse those people who took all her money so that in the end she was short of hospital fees? Why don't they blame those men who ill-treated her? Why only Kamal Amrohi?

'Today I know that Meena never loved me. All her life she kept acting with me. And like a fool I fell for it. Now she has gone and left her diaries with an outside person, not her sister which I could have overlooked. How could she do it?' He paused. 'Do you know I can't even complain to her. Allah! What a game.'

I didn't believe him but he told me, 'Before she died I still loved her, but today there is no room for that woman in my heart.'

The reader must have noticed by now my sympathy for Amrohi—a sympathy which initially began as a reaction to the general press verdict that he was the villain in the Meena Kumari story.

Reports, appreciations, relatives all contributed in making Amrohi appear as the ogre who destroyed my heroine.

The reason they did this was because Meena's private life was like a Hindi film, and therefore it demanded a nice, rounded, simple ending. To complete this story a 'bad guy' was needed, and one who was perfect for this role, considering all that had been said about him in the past, was Amrohi.

I carry no brief to whitewash Chandan. I know him purely because of this book, and if I had found him to be the assassin I would not have hesitated to join the popular chorus.

Incidentally, I don't think he was the ideal husband, but then my heroine was not the ideal wife.

I come back now to the query I raised earlier and left in the air. It relates to my heroine's sense of restriction. What was the nature of this freedom she was looking for?

I am now in such deep, delicate, treacherous waters that each step I take must be sure-footed. Circumspectly therefore I am going to bring in the open an area in Meena Kumari's life which has hitherto only been gossiped and scandalized. It deserves better.

Common knowledge: Meena Kumari was in pursuit of love. And being an ordinary human woman, love for her was not merely the holding of hands, the recitation of poetry, the eye-gazing: it had its physical side too. My heroine's concept of love included a blending of the mental and the physical. Seldom was she able to find both.

In temperament and disposition I am not very close to Meena Kumari, but if there is one area where I agree with her wholeheartedly, unreservedly and totally, it is in her understanding of love.

As a country we are renowned hypocrites over love and sex,

and Meena was a magnificent exception in as much that she
was completely honest and uncompromising.

Sometimes, and there is no use denying this, the requirements
of the flesh ran away with her and she found herself with men
with whom she had little rapport. Loneliness, we all know,
makes for strange bedfellows.

But this is too simplistic and perhaps untrue a statement;
because to understand Meena Kumari you have to understand
Mahajabeen—the four-year-old girl clinging to a profession
where indecency and immorality is a way of life.

Let us however go back even further. Mahajabeen was
born into a family where subsistence was first priority, and the
owners of this family had no interest in progeny unless they
were of financial use to them.

How miserable, decrepit, unhappy and unloved a childhood
Mahajabeen had is difficult to convey. In India there are
millions of people living on the subsistence level and the Buxs
were no exception; the only difference existed in the fact that
Ali Bux and Iqbal Begum were determined to improve their
status. However, they did not wish to achieve this by their
own genius, but by exploiting their daughter. Indeed, the first
people to use my heroine were none other than her parents.

Mahajabeen, remember, was unwanted anyway. (The Ali
Buxs desired a son.) And till the time that her moneymaking
potential was spotted, she received extremely shabby and
psychologically damaging treatment.

Around 1936, Khursheed, as far as the family was concerned,
was the favourite daughter due to her earning capabilities (she
was a child star). Consequently, all attention and favour was
showered on her, and Mahajabeen watched this partiality from
the sidelines. My heroine wore her sister's clothes, she never

got the chocolates Khursheed got (Meena was dead keen on sweets); she had an interest in books but the mother made sure that this interest was sidetracked; she had a friend—someone called Shamim—with whom she enjoyed sitting and talking, but this young friendship was scotched.

'I thought she did not love me ... she was very much disappointed when I was born as, I was told later, she wanted a son. When I grew up she used to tell me that I was a good-for-nothing girl and I would not be able to do anything in life ... the atmosphere in which I grew up was devoid of love and affection, at least that is what I felt as a child. Since then I am looking for love, searching for it, craving for it.'

Mahajabeen's primary business was to earn a living for her parents and nothing was allowed to interfere with this business. I am no psychiatrist but this stilted, loveless, mercenary early experience surely had disastrous moulding consequences on my heroine.

Officially the Ali Bux–Iqbal Begum marriage was successful; unofficially the atmosphere at home was far from congenial. Mahajabeen's parents were frequently quarrelling and worse, in front of the children. The subject of the rows: money.

Thus, love, the birthright of every unorphaned child, was denied to Mahajabeen. But perhaps more importantly, peace and domestic calm were denied to her.

Kamal Amrohi told me that when he met his nineteen-year-old Manju at Sassoon Hospital, Poona, he found her to be a remarkably mature, clear-thinking person. Similarly, even at the age of seven or eight she was able to see with great clarity the sort of treatment meted out to her, and why.

You can imagine how she felt a few years later when she became the money-spinner, and her parents' behaviour was reversed. Then she became the idol, the favourite child and all her whims and caprices were indulged—no shortage of chocolates now!

Thus, from a tender age she was used, exploited, and from an early age she learned her most memorable lesson: trust no one.

Not many people know this but my heroine was mulishly obstinate—about trivialities, invariably. 'Sometimes in some remote place she would ask for pineapple juice, and create hell if she didn't get it. It was no use trying to explain to her that pineapple juice was not available here. It was no use trying to pacify her with something else. No, she wanted pineapple juice and it didn't matter whether she paid 10,000 rupees, but she wanted it.' This was told to me by someone who accompanied my heroine on her travels. Khursheed put it more succinctly, 'If she wanted something, she went and got it.'

Most reasonable people accept that early environment is largely responsible for shaping future personality, character and attitudes; and so it was in the case of Meena Kumari.

One doesn't therefore have to be Freud to see the link between Mahajabeen's obstinacy and Mahajabeen's early life.

I promised earlier that I would attempt to explain why my heroine in her professional life preferred sorrow to laughter; preferred the tragedienne to the comedienne. I don't think that explanation is necessary now. If you know about Meena Kumari's Dadar and Bandra home days, you will see quite clearly why she felt more at ease with tears.

Since she was deprived of love, she overestimated and over-exaggerated its significance as a therapy. Meena Kumari was a wise, sapient human being, yet when it came to love she was like a starry-eyed schoolgirl expecting too much and always finding too little.

This is understandable. Those who are unfulfilled emotionally have a tendency to view love as some kind of panacea—something which will provide an answer to all the ills of life. Conversely, if this love is not found, for them, all life, however rewarding in other spheres, is meaningless.

And of course Urdu poetry is notorious for advancing this version, and you know how heavily my heroine was under the sedation of this sort of verse.

The cumulative impact of this was that Meena Kumari was never able to find sufficient love. Because she gave every inch of herself she expected the same measure in return. Further, the commitment in her case was so total, the hunger so voracious, the passion so overwhelming, that she soon felt dissatisfied. 'Many a time I thought that my destination was within my reach and I was going to get that love for which I was longing, but again and again, I realized, though late, that I was running after a "mirage".'

Boredom as a determining factor in the lives of those who are said to be promiscuous has been both maligned and neglected. Because she was an engaging and diverting person herself, Meena Kumari got quickly bored with her men.

The truth, the harsh bitter truth, is that people exhaust each other. Irresistible on Monday, Interesting on Tuesday, Tolerable on Wednesday, Dull on Thursday, Insufferable on Friday—this is usually the cycle of human relationship.

My heroine left Amrohi because she no longer loved him. And one of the reasons she no longer loved him was because he had become for her a less interesting person. When she met him in 1951, she was overawed by him; when she left him in 1964 he bored her. (Amrohi's only film after he married Meena was *Daera*, a miserable flop, and the fate of the much-publicized *Pakeezah* hung in balance.) Meena felt that she was married to a nonentity, a man who as an artiste was way past his prime. (This impression, I understand, was altered after she saw the completed *Pakeezah*, and she told a friend that she was convinced that her husband was the finest film-maker in India.)

Could Amrohi have saved his marriage? Could he have become more interesting for his wife? Could he have given her the intensity and quantity of love she required? I am afraid not. In fact, very few people could have held my heroine's attention for long—which, please note, is intended as a compliment to her.

Some people close to my heroine maintain that Dharmendra, not Amrohi, was the most important man in her life. They say I have got my positioning wrong. The Meena Kumari sisters for example are quite convinced that Dharam 'was the only man she loved'.

I am not entirely sure whether this is true; what I am sure about is that Meena—even after she had stopped seeing Dharmendra—had great regard for him.

There were two reasons for this:

One, Mr Dharam was her protege, her pupil. She had helped him enormously in the initial stages of his career, and she took legitimate pride when he made good. Dharam himself has never tried to minimize the debt he owes to Meena for making him what he is today.

Two, he was among the very few men who were genuinely good to her. In real life I believe he is a thoroughly decent and unpretentious guy, and he thought a lot of my heroine. (Each time he went to see her in Landmark he would come out of her room crying. Khursheed once asked him why. 'I can't help it,' was his simple and honest reply.)

The popular view is that Meena and Dharam were intimate for three years. The inside view is that the intimacy lasted no more than six months.

While it lasted, however, it glittered and in six months this couple had given rise to rumours enough for many years.

No denying that Dharam enjoyed the limelight. He was an unknown boy and his liaison with India's foremost actress got him a lot of gratis publicity. Most of the time he was visibly at her side, and when he was not, he made sure this news travelled.

He had gone to Delhi for the premiere of *Kaajal*, and at some party there downed a couple of excess drinks. When he arrived at the airport the authorities noticing his inebriated state refused to let him in the plane. 'But I must get back to Bombay. I must,' he entreated, 'Meena is waiting for me.' This statement and incident were faithfully reported in the press the next day.

My heroine did not fall short either. She had gone in a convoy to a picnic with lots of friends among whom was Mr Dharmendra. While returning, somehow Dharam got inside a different car from Meena and whisked away. She was hysterical. She wanted to know why he wasn't in the car beside her. She wanted to know whether he had run away. She wanted to know if possibly something had happened to him. The other picnickers assured that all was well with Dharam and through an oversight he had left in one of the other cars. But this assurance wasn't enough. Meena directed the driver of her car to stop. He did. Coolly she got out of the car and went on to the middle of the road. Here, cross-legged, she sat and began lamenting loudly, 'Where is my Dharam? Where is my Dharam?'

If you were involved with Meena, that automatically meant you were involved in fairy-tale fiction. Dharam received his share. A slapping incident is rumoured, a full-scale fist fight between Mrs Dharmendra and my heroine in Srinagar is rumoured, a couple of drinking incidents in which Meena had to stabilize her man are rumoured.

Most, if not all of these, can be dismissed. These incidents are the work of fertile unemployed minds. Mr Dharmendra by all accounts is a gentleman, a veritable Sir Galahad, and I can't see him slapping my heroine.

More relevant is whether he used her, and whether his interest in Meena Kumari was stimulated from the very beginning by his cinema ambition.

The film mags and press have all made a case against Dharmendra. 'He pretended to be in love with her as long as it suited him. Once he had established himself, with Meena's aid, he did not care to look at her.' It would appear he has been cast as Villain No. 2 in the Meena Kumari tragedy.

I think there is truth in this charge. But of a different sort. He did use her; however, never deliberately or malignantly. And he definitely did not leave her for the reason popularly suggested.

Meena, it must be remembered, sought Dharmendra and not the other way round. So the question of a preconceived Dharmendra plan to use Meena does not arise. Further, at the time Meena sought, he was not fully obscure. He had made a few films—nothing extraordinary—which had placed him in the eyes of both the public and the producers.

One advantage he admittedly made good use of was the spin-off publicity and renown he got by being constantly at

Meena's side (I believe in 1964 he was introduced around as 'Meena Kumari's friend'). Producers, directors, financiers noted this with professional alacrity and some of them must have reasoned like this: 'Since Meena Kumari is constantly with this young man, and since Meena Kumari appears to be extremely fond of him, it would be a good idea to include this man in films in which Meena Kumari's services are being negotiated.' These were the sort of considerations that Dharmendra benefited from.

Film-makers who were not too receptive to the idea of using him were directly and discreetly pressurized to do so by my heroine. But let this be clearly understood, Meena did this entirely on her own accord and not at Dharam's asking. She was resolved that her pupil should redeem her confidence, and she continued to get him as many opportunities as possible. A glance at the Meena Kumari films between 1964 and 1967 will give substance to my contention.

Fortunately, after the success of *Phool Aur Patthar* there wasn't great need for pressure; both these people were now a 'winning romantic team'.

So much mutual concern, so much mutual love, so much mutual affection didn't work? Yes, in six months the foundations of the Meena-Dharam association lay shattered.

On the surface the reasons seem at once obvious and inescapable. Mr Dharmendra was a married man, thus the impermanence of the liaison was always understood—at least by the two romantics directly concerned. My heroine demanded devotion and devotion demanded time. The increasingly popular and ruggedly handsome man found he couldn't spend as many hours at Janki Kutir as before. Additionally, his brothers and family warned him that they would not put up with neglect any more. He was required to tend to his wife and his son.

My own view is that these were minor matters. They were supposed to be in love after all and none of the difficulties mentioned above are insurmountable for people in that state of bliss. No, something more fundamental was wrong which was eating away at the roots of the relationship.

Dharmendra never loved Meena. Never loved her as a woman. He revered her. He worshipped her. For him she was a mighty actress, and correspondingly he had placed her on a royal pedestal. To be near her was enough; to touch her was possibly sacrilege.

My heroine was uncomfortable on pedestals. She had both her feet on the ground and she loved Dharam as any normal woman loves a man. Thus they both loved, but there was a discrepancy in spirit and passion. It turned out to be fatal.

I can't help placing a literary parallel here. The Dharam–Meena romantic team reminds me very much of another romantic team immortalized by D.H. Lawrence: Mellors and Lady Chatterley. Meena Kumari saw in her man the same qualities of honesty, robustness and loyalty that her Ladyship saw in her man.

That leaves only Gulzar in the loves of Meena Kumari. Ostensibly, he should have been her most important man, since she fought over him at *Pinjre Ke Panchhi* and took the monumental step of leaving Kamal's house after a stay of twelve years.

I had a rather unhappy session with Gulzar. With most of the others I was able to establish my credentials as a serious biographer, and they were invariably helpful. Mr Gulzar was evasive to say the least and continually tried to divert me with generalities and non-statements.

One phrase he used seemed typical of this: 'We used to share artistic moments together.' I questioned him time and time again on how close he was to my heroine, and each time, almost like a stopper, he said, 'We used to share artistic moments together.' Secretly, I said to myself, 'I bet you did more than that.'

Today I feel I have been unfair to Gulzar. It is just possible that they did share those moments and nothing else. Although the director of *Mere Apne* is officially included among the Meena Kumari lovers, his was a more platonic love. My heroine admired his writing qualities and later his directorial acumen (she thought very highly of *Mere Apne*). Also, in the last months Gulzar came back into the picture and revived an old association. She was thankful for this revival.

Meena, I think, used him. In 1964 she did. Poor Gulzar had no idea of the whirlwind in store for him on 5 March at the mahurat. And no person was more surprised than him at the part he played going up the stairs. He always knew that Meena had regard for him, but he had never anticipated that she would be prepared to leave her home rather than forfeit the right to sit with him in her make-up room.

Actually, he was no more than a convenient excuse—'a stool pigeon'. Meena was guilty of deceiving him. Understandably, after the flare-up, he thought Meena was in love with him, and he expected this relationship to continue and flower. Much to his chagrin a few weeks after 5 March, Mr Dharmendra appeared on the scene and my heroine had no time now to share artistic moments with Gulzar.

Chivalrously and magnanimously, he remained loyal to her and it must be acknowledged that in her hour of need he came back and offered whatever solace he could. The diaries that Meena left him were primarily a token of thanks for his loyalty. Possibly my heroine felt that this was one man she had not been scrupulously fair with and he thus deserved her most intimate and cherished possession—her diaries.

No one except Mr Gulzar knows the exact contents of these diaries—the ones that Amrohi covets. There is a feeling that my heroine has spilled the beans. 'Every single man and woman who used Meena has been brought into the open,' says someone who claims to know the details.

I asked Gulzar the flavour of the pages in his possession. He wasn't very helpful. I persisted and enquired if they were vindictive and whether Meena had really spilled the beans. 'No,' he replied, 'she wasn't that sort of person.'

A couple of pages from these diaries I have read (Gulzar released them to a magazine), and they are very much like her poetry. In other words they are sad and descriptive. Mountains, rivers, mornings, trivial happenings are all evoked in a language which is deeply introspective. However, I would be the last to state that this is all the diaries have. Maybe Gulzar has been selective and reserved all the fireworks for the biography which he is planning to write.

There were other men in my heroine's life. Prominent among them are Rahul and Sawan Kumar. Personally I don't attach much importance (no disrespect intended) to them as far as the direction of Meena Kumari's life is concerned. By the time she met them, her views and attitudes were determined and clearly chalked.

If men played a significant part in Meena's life, so did her relatives. 'They destroyed her' was a proposition put to me many times and substantiated with examples.

The quality of Meena Kumari's kith and kin may be open

to dispute but not their quantity. Sisters, stepsisters, brothers-in-law, nephews, nieces, cousins—they made up a mighty number and she was accessible to them all, and all of these people lived with my heroine off and on.

Go and meet them in their houses and each will give you his version. They hang up large pictures of Meena around which they burn incense and throw garlands. 'She is the only thing that mattered in my life,' they all say.

Yet I know Meena had a love-hate relationship with her relatives. In fact she never thought much of them. Alas, she was alone and needed them—needed them physically.

After she left Amrohi and set up house herself she required people to run the house, she required family company. However, when they began exceeding their position, when they tried to control her life, she quarrelled with them and kicked them out. On one occasion she even solicited the services of the police to remove somebody from her house.

What sort of people are Khursheed, Madhu, Shama, Osman, Altaf, Kishore Sharma? The things I have heard about them I would hesitate to put on paper (simply because there is no way I can confirm them). If even a fraction of what I have been told is true, my heroine is better off where she is today.

All families are distinctive, but the Ali Bux family is extraordinarily distinctive. I have met some members of this clan and I must confess they are all fascinating people. 'All great actors', to use Kishore Sharma's words. And each member of this clan has a watertight story about his involvement with my heroine. When I used to come back after seeing one of them I would say to myself: 'So-and-so has been maligned,' and congratulate myself for having at last found a person who cared and loved Meena Kumari. Of course the next visit to some other relative put paid to all that.

I regret if this sentence sounds like a dialogue from a bad Hindi film, but poverty makes people do many things. Meena Kumari's kith and kin were uniformly impoverished and they all looked towards their one relative who had made it. Their own chance of making it depended solely on the generosity of Meena and they spared no pains to ingratiate themselves with her.

It would be a harsh and idealistic man who would criticize such behaviour. No one in this world loves anybody altruistically. Meena Kumari's cousins loved her with a purpose. And make no mistake, Meena Kumari knew this. She once confided that she was convinced that whoever she lived with was going to use her; so why not her relatives.

Supposing my heroine's relatives had been financially secure, would their behaviour have been any different? I would like to believe so—after all they are human beings gifted with decent human qualities. As I now think back to them I feel at heart they are all good people contaminated by the world's most powerful and fearful contaminator, money. If Meena Kumari had been born in the Tata household her life story would have been different.

What verdict then on the proposition that Meena Kumari was destroyed by her relatives? This one-man jury after examining the evidence pronounces 'not guilty'.

My heroine exhausts me. I am now going to spend a page or so scrutinizing her will which she made on 6 March 1972. The attention I devote to this document will necessarily be inadequate, even a 100-pager would be inadequate. The ramifications of this will, the twists and turns of plot are worthy of the talents of Inspector Eagle.

Let me begin with the salient points of the will. My heroine left a sizable portion of wealth to the Lions Club (Landmark flat, Pali Hill land interest and moneys to come from films). She desired that a trust be set up in her name and the income used for helping the blind. Her flat in Khar she gave to Khursheed. The income from her bank deposits, from the sale of her Polydor record, from her two cars, from any moneys realized when and if her official biography is written she bequeathed to a Shia education trust. Her personal effects (jewellery, clothes, etc.) she divided among her relatives.

The first point about this will is that it is new. My heroine had previously made out a document which she superseded in favour of this new one. The second point relates to the education of Shias. Meena Kumari was a Sunni, and although she was totally secular in her beliefs, the question can be asked, why Shia education and not Sunni?

I think this is all part of my heroine's benign mischief and she did this partly to confuse me and partly to tantalize Amrohi.

Mr Sharma is of the opinion that this new will is counterfeit since it ignores and has not taken into account many assets which only he and Meena knew. He also feels that this document is loaded too heavily towards Khursheed. I refuse to make any comment on this.

What I will comment on however is Meena Kumari's income tax.

My heroine died a debtor. Currently she owes five lakh rupees to the Government of India, and all her property has been confiscated. In legal language all of Meena Kumari's worldly possessions are 'attached property'. Unless the income tax authorities waive their dues or unless some money is found, my heroine's philanthropic intentions will never get off the ground. The money realized from her property will go to the taxman.

One solution Meena's followers talk about concerns Mr Amrohi. The feeling is that he should step in and offer to make good the tax deficit. He should do this as a gesture to his Manju, and as some sort of payment for Manju's contribution to *Pakeezah*. Amrohi says he sees no reason to do this. Since his wife was living away from him and since he was not connected with her financial affairs, all this is none of his business.

Incidentally, another feeling, less noble, says that Meena Kumari's will is nothing else but a public relations trick. The writers of this last testament were fully aware that the Lions Club and Shia trusts would never be in a position to be worked. However, the gesture would be noted and widely acclaimed. If all Meena's money goes to income tax, people will hardly forget that she intended it to go to better places.

Whether this is true or not, only Allah, fittingly, knows. I can only state that if it is, my heroine had no hand in it.

A person who is very active in the deliberation of the trusts and the will is Nargis Dutt. I met her one morning while she was breakfasting (poached eggs and fruit juice) and she had all sorts of plans to ensure that every single line of the will was adhered to. 'I have written to the prime minister,' she said, 'asking her to waive Meena's income tax dues. So far I have received no reply. I am going to Delhi to see her personally.' Nargis was particularly agitated that everyone, including me, was using my heroine. 'How many people in India know she died a debtor? And how many people are doing anything about this?'

Those involved in the will and those involved with my heroine do not look with favour on Nargis. Although Meena and Nargis were good friends, the view is that Nargis is unnecessarily interfering in business which is no concern of hers. Uncharitably she is referred to as the 'Indira Gandhi of the film world'. Mrs Dutt, people say, lacks lucrative and interesting occupation these days and consequently is looking for opportunities to throw her weight around. 'Why doesn't she stick to opening exhibitions,' was one comment.

In my judgement, Mrs Dutt's interference is entirely warranted. I would much rather trust her than some of the others I have seen.

It is difficult to compass the exact date, but around 1962 Meena lost faith and hope in the future. She realized she was not going to find her style of love. Therefore she concluded she would take things as they came. Personal relationships were for her satisfying and worthwhile if they provided cursory cheer—no more was expected, and no more was usually received.

I fancy she took the same attitude towards the bottle. If brandy or whatever else she was drinking was successful in short-term clouding and fuzzing of her difficulties, it was essential and useful. Never did she wait to consider such mundane things like the effect of 9.00 a.m. brandy drinking.

I doubt if she ever seriously thought about what was in store for her the next day or the next week or the next month. The present was of consequence, the future indeterminate and hence negligible.

As a result she began life on a day-to-day basis. Sometimes she would meet someone promising and there would be brief hopeless hope that something enduring had been discovered, but very soon she received knowledge, that like before, this was wishful thinking.

From 1962 onwards a modus vivendi had been agreed. She decided to divide herself into various compartments. There was her professional life, there was her intellectual life, there was her business life, there was her love life. For each of these compartments she had appropriate companions, and she made sure none of the compartments overlapped or clashed.

For example, if her association with you was professional, and you called on her while she was drinking she would keep you waiting a few minutes. In that period she would get all traces of alcohol removed and receive you in her chamber on the accepted basis. There are many people who knew my heroine intimately, visited her frequently, and they swear they have never seen her drunk or drink.

Arbitrarily, if you on your own accord decided to cross from one compartment to another she would snub you with all the venom of a cobra. My heroine was gentle and kind but there were certain areas where she was going to stand no nonsense.

Some comment on my heroine's lifestyle is called for. By butchering herself into parts, Meena was hoping to reconcile her vital needs. On the face of it this was astute. If she couldn't find one human being intelligent or decent or good enough, she thought she would employ a whole gang of people, and perhaps collectively find what she was looking for individually.

If you know her past, you cannot censure such a mode of existence. My heroine was simply making a compromise, simply trying to tie up the ends of what seemed an impossible heartache.

I feel the compromise was neither happy nor successful. It couldn't be—since the nature of the compromise was repulsive to Meena Kumari.

The longer she lived with her mode of life in Janki Kutir, in

Landmark, in Rembrandt, the more apparent it became to her that it was wretched and possibly immoral. If only she had the strength to turn away, to accept the mortifying and killing truth that in the most crucial area of her life (the physical-emotional) she would remain, for all time, unfulfilled.

Now if Meena had been Joan of Arc or Mother Teresa or Sita she would have laughingly accepted the realities of her fate. But Meena Kumari was no saint. I repeat, no saint. Had she been one she would have quietly continued her vocation, and you and I would have been immeasurably poorer. For myself I know I would not have written this book with the joy and earnestness I have if Meena had died of fever or of old age.

'I confess that I was never a goddess. I am not a goddess and I don't intend to be one. I confess that I am not the ideal woman whom you often see on the screen. No, I am just a woman who wants to live, who wants to love, and who wants to be loved,' is her own honest assessment.

Like in all mystery stories—and if ever there was a mystery story it was my heroine's—we now come to the rub. Who did it, or what did it? Who killed Meena Kumari?

Let us summon the line-up of the accused: Amrohi, Dharmendra, assorted lovers, brandy, relatives, Filmfare Awards. One person, however, is missing in this line-up, and that person is Meena Kumari. Before you tear this book into a thousand pieces listen to the voice of the woman herself: 'For me a bad woman means a weak woman and I am a weak woman. I have many weaknesses, many faults, many shortcomings. But somehow in my loneliest and saddest moments, when I want to run away from the whole world and be with myself to blame or pity myself, I have never thought that Meena Kumari is evil. But bad she is, a bundle of weaknesses.'

She lies. She is not and was never a bad woman. Rather she was a towering and inspiring specimen of a human being gloriously and beautifully invested in mortal flesh. Two thousand years ago they crucified a bearded man in Jerusalem because they said he was 'evil'. Today, and for many years, we know he wasn't evil; and today what millions worship is not so much his divinity but his humanity.

I do not ask you to worship Meena Kumari but to understand her; and if you have, you must join me in proclaiming that she was not only a great actress but a great human being. If you are inhuman, if you are cruel, if you believe in saints and sinners, I ask you to forget Meena Kumari the woman and remember Meena Kumari the film star, the actress.

The writer of this book however stands by what he wrote on its front page, 'Wish I had known you.'

Index